Unfuck Your Worth

OVERCOME YOUR MONEY EMOTIONS, VALUE YOUR OWN LABOR, AND MANAGE FINANCIAL FREAK-OUTS IN A CAPITALIST HELLSCAPE

FAITH G. HARPER,
PhD, LPC-S, ACS, ACN

MICROCOSM PUBLISHING
Portland, Ore

T0001564

UNFUCK YOUR WORTH: *Overcome Your Money Emotions, Value Your Own Labor, and Manage Financial Freak-outs in a Capitalist Hellscape*

Part of the 5 Minute Therapy Series
© Dr. Faith Harper, 2020
First edition © Microcosm Publishing, August 25, 2020
ISBN 978-1-62106-456-5
This is Microcosm #313
Edited by Elly Blue and Lydia Rogue
Design by Joe Biel

Illustrations by River Katz

For a catalog, write or visit:
Microcosm Publishing
2752 N Williams Ave.
Portland, OR 97227

www.Microcosm.Pub

To join the ranks of high-class stores that feature Microcosm titles, talk to your rep: In the U.S. **Como** (Atlantic), **Fujii** (Midwest), **Book Travelers West** (Pacific), **Turnaround** in Europe, **Manda/UTP** in Canada, **New South** in Australia, and **GPS** in Asia, India, Africa, and South America. We are sold by **Gifts of Nature** in the gift market.

Did you know that you can buy our books directly from us at sliding scale rates? Support a small, independent publisher and pay less than Amazon's price at www. **Microcosm.Pub**

Library of Congress Cataloging-in-Publication Data
Names: Harper, Faith G., author.
Title: Unfuck your worth : manage your money emotions, value your own
  labor, and manage financial freak-outs in a capitalist hellscape / by
  Faith G. Harper, PhD, LPC-S, ACS, ACN.
Description: Portland, OR : Microcosm Publishing, 2020. | Summary:
  "Untangle your emotions and expectations about money so that you can
  live your best financial life. Without fear and shame holding you back,
  it's more possible to move past all those social barriers to actualizing
  whatever your money aspirations are, whether that's getting a raise,
  getting out of debt, having honest conversations about money with your
  family, raising your kids to be savers, or wherever your values lead
  you. Dr. Faith, author of the bestselling Unf*ck Your Brain and Unf*ck
  Your Intimacy, tackles one of the toughest emotional topics there is
  with her trademark mix of neuroscience, gentle encouragement, and
  no-nonsense language. This book isn't about getting rich quick (or
  necessarily at all)-it's about figuring out your own economic values and
  baggage, and learning to be the person in the world you know you have it
  in you to be"-- Provided by publisher.
Identifiers: LCCN 2019058729 (print) | LCCN 2019058730 (ebook) | ISBN
  9781621064565 (paperback) | ISBN 9781621061885 (ebook)
Subjects: LCSH: Finance, Personal. | Money--Social aspects. | Human
  capital.
Classification: LCC HG179 .H3175 2020 (print) | LCC HG179 (ebook) | DDC
  332.024--dc23
LC record available at https://lccn.loc.gov/2019058729
LC ebook record available at https://lccn.loc.gov/2019058730

MICROCOSM·PUBLISHING

Microcosm Publishing is Portland's most diversified publishing house and distributor with a focus on the colorful, authentic, and empowering. Our books and zines have put your power in your hands since 1996, equipping readers to make positive changes in their lives and in the world around them. Microcosm emphasizes skill-building, showing hidden histories, and fostering creativity through challenging conventional publishing wisdom with books and bookettes about DIY skills, food, bicycling, gender, self-care, and social justice. What was once a distro and record label was started by Joe Biel in his bedroom and has become among the oldest independent publishing houses in Portland, OR. We are a politically moderate, centrist publisher in a world that has inched to the right for the past 80 years.

Global labor conditions are bad, and our roots in industrial Cleveland in the 70s and 80s made us appreciate the need to treat workers right. Therefore, our books are MADE IN THE USA.

Contents

Introduction

Money is emotional. It's scary. And complicated. And gross. Our interactions with it generally feel shitty.

But this shittiness is a mostly-unspoken truth about money. All of the many lovely, pragmatic financial planning books we buy end up gathering dust because we don't *feel* pragmatic about money. Then, because we have assigned it a central focus in our lives, in this weird, theoretical, culturally-agreed-upon way, we get fucked up about it. The worth we assign to ourselves and others gets tied into our experiences with money.

Money can make us sad and scared. And shitty and mean. And frustrated and self-recriminating and avoidant.

Nothing brings out our worst selves more than money does. Well, that and sex. But I already wrote that book.

Why does money fuck us up so badly? A lot of it has to do with trauma, both individual and societal. A lot of it has to do with capitalism. The way we are fucked up about money makes us equate our worth as people with our class or our income or the size of our house or car, or our savings or our clothes or our job or our ability to work. Money makes us forget our true worth, which has nothing to do with money.

Ultimately, the way to unfuck our worth is to understand that *money is energy*. Not in a magic, woo-woo kind of way but in material terms of time, labor, and communication. Thinking about money as energy that we expend, take in, exchange, or share, instead of as a barometer of our worth helps overcome the trauma. So does supporting each other as we do this hard, scary work.

· · ·

Most books about money focus on just one way to relate with your finances. Generally like saving the fuck out of every penny (*All coffee must be made at home, what the fuck is your problem you five dollar latte drinker?*) or on investing in a particular way (usually with an investment program or course written by the author). Or they tell you to harness the power of your mind to bring wealth to you (attitude is important, I agree, but this kind of toxic victim blaming is giving me perpetual muppet stank face). Or all of the above.

I'm frustrated by these books, and I'm guessing you are, too. While so many of these books remain stupid-popular despite having been debunked (I am looking directly at you, *Rich Dad, Poor Dad*), more and more people are wising up to the fact that the only financial difference they are making in our lives is that the 20 bucks we spent on the damn thing made us 20 dollars poorer.

So how is this book different?

This book is about our emotional relationship with money and how it's influenced by fucking trauma and other brain-wiring survival instincts. It's about how the value of a dollar becomes equated with the value of our personhood. And about how all of those issues make it seem utterly out of reach to even think about creating a workable budget and getting ahead in ways that are meaningful to you.

Because if you are fucked up about money that means the system is working.

Conflating the value of your personhood with the money in your pocket? Operating from a place of trauma-influenced chaos? Carrying tons of debt? Paying tons of interest? Spending money in ways that advertisers tell you will make you feel better instead of in ways that actually make you feel better? Any or all of the above means the current economic system makes mad bank off of you. And then it tells you it's your fault that your shit isn't together. As long as we all believe that to be true, the capitalist hellscape mentioned in the title of the book stays alive. And I'm so over all of that, what about you?

So obviously we are gonna get into the "hey, budgets are important and shit!" part of the program, but first we really need to get into money, worth, culture, society, and brain science.

A lot of the issues that most of us have around money are due to large scale problems in our greater culture *and* the fact that our brains are trying to make sense of a concept that is actually quite intangible. In terms of evolution, our brains are not nearly caught up with the world we live in, which is a product of the industrial revolution.

And it shows. It shows in our culture's wealth disparity. It shows in our multigenerational financial struggles. It shows in the dumb shit we do with money. It shows in what we value and center in terms of worth.

If we don't know what we are fighting against, we are absolutely going to fail. So let's talk about all the shit that's getting us in trouble, okay?

Wouldn't it be cool if a book looked at how the brain is wired to work, and how that is impacted by how our current culture actually operates, *and* how that jacks up our habits of mind about money and worth and value?

What if we approached budgeting as radical self care built on the value system of the person reading the book, not the person writing it?

And, *holy shit*, what if we straight up owned how fucked up late-stage capitalism is and used that reality as a framework for discussing all of the things we are struggling with, like asking for a raise, deciding whether or not to monetize our creative endeavors, investing in higher education, investing in wealth portfolios, or getting off the damn grid all together.

I didn't think I would have any excitement about writing a book about money, but I really loved writing this one. It's the book I wish my 20 year old self had, but my 45 year old self is also thrilled to have.

There is also an accompanying workbook, since y'all are a bunch of hard-core, do-all-the-unfuckening-things, ass-kicking world changers. You don't need the workbook for the book to make sense (or vice-versa) but they complement each other really well, because the workbook has additional budgeting worksheets, money value tools, and all that fancy jazz.

Money discussions are typically pretty painful and shaming. Due in no small part to the fact that we are supposed to be taking personal responsibility for a broken system. But we've already decided to stop telling ourselves that story, right? And while doing hard work can still be painful (yaaay adulting), shame has zero place here. And as you read forward you will see why more and more.

If Money Were a Person, Who Would Your Person Be?

Okay, let's be honest. Money may be abstract, but it's an abstract thing that has a hugely tangible effect on your life, right? You are interacting with money as much as you are with the human beings in your life (unless you are completely, awesomely off the grid). So let's give your money the persona it honestly has anyway.

Think about these questions. Write down your answers if you want. If writing directly in a book horrifies you, use that cool journal you bought that you've been saving for a "special" project. This is totally special, crack that bitch open.

Consider these questions:

- Do you and money get along well?

- What is the nature of your relationship?

- What do you think about money?

- How do you feel about money?

- How does money treat you?

- How do you treat money?

PART ONE

HOW OUR WORTH GETS FUCKED UP

First of all, what do I even mean by worth? I don't mean the amount in your bank account.

"Worth" is one of those words that is generally poorly defined, and often conflated with self-esteem. Self-esteem is defined by what you do or don't do, how you succeed or don't succeed. Getting a promotion? Generally good for self-esteem. Getting fired? Generally bad. Financial wealth? Definitely in the plus category for self-esteem, while being broke will shit-can self esteem pretty quickly. And here is where worth comes in.

Self-worth is about who we are, not what we do. It's the sum total of the value of your personhood, as defined by you.

We live in a toxic system in which self-esteem has become entirely conflated with self-worth. One study conducted by the University of Michigan Institute for Social Research found that our pursuit of worth through esteem caused issues with stress, anger, school and job performance, eating disorders, drug and alcohol problems, and problems with interpersonal relationships (both romantic and platonic).

Self-esteem is the total of our self-rating system. When we have more in the minus column than the plus column, it bottoms out. But when we shift into just *being* ourselves instead of *rating* ourselves, we have a self-worth that is centered away from plusses and minuses. We find that we have worth outside of our income bracket, our debt ratio, our job titles, and the other ways we measure self-esteem. We have value and worth because we are human beings with *intrinsic* value and worth. This is hard to remember in a system that tells you that you must be above average in all ways—a statistical improbability—to have intrinsic value and worth.

You've heard the expression *"Money is the root of all evil,"* right? So, preacher's kid here to tell you that's not exactly what 1 Timothy 6:10 actually says. Let's be accurate, shall we? (And then that's the last bible verse, I promise.)

> *For the love of money is a root of all kinds of evils. It is through this craving that some have wandered away from the faith and pierced themselves with many pangs.*

Ye olde-timey language saying the exact same thing as I am: Money isn't the problem. The conflation of money and worth is what is beating the shit out of us, day in and day out.

In the first part of this book, we're going to look at how these *piercings* and *pangs* play out in everyday life. We'll talk about how the concept of money doesn't overlap particularly well with how human brains work. We'll get into addiction stuff, because not every bad spending habit is an actual addiction (and treating it like one creates a lot of frustration and failure). And of course we'll spend some time looking at how society works and why *that* is a problem. And most of all, we'll go through how trauma impacts our relationship with money and how to get better. Because we may not be able to stop capitalism, but we can heal from trauma.

But before we get into it, here's a tool to help.

The COAL Trick

We are going to talk about money and brain fuckery and all the things that fuck us up and kick our self-esteem in the teeth in a minute. That can be really activating for anyone who has struggled with their self-worth. So I have a little trick for that which can really help.

Losing track of our self-worth means we end up taking judgmental stances against ourselves. We get into a negative spin of self-recrimination and beating up on ourselves, even being hard on ourselves *for* being hard on ourselves.

The trick is to approach these thoughts and feelings with curiosity instead of judgement. Like, "Oh, hey, I wonder what that's about?"

Dan Siegal uses the acronym COAL, which expands on the same idea. COAL stands for:

Curiosity

Openness

Acceptance

Love

So as you read this book, if you find yourself getting anxious or upset, remember COAL and see if you can disrupt the cycle of feeling bad about feeling bad. Also? Notice what you're upset about because that's probably where you can do the best work.

When we start approaching our own minds with this level of respect, we recenter our worth. This is good shit. It takes practice. Like, a lot of practice. But it helps us keep our worth in its rightful place while we do all the heavy unfuckening work.

Internalized Messaging Check-In

Let's take a minute to see how money specifically is influencing your self-worth, okay?

Complete the following sentences with your own answers:

- Poor people are . . .

- Rich people are . . .

- I am . . .

We all create internal "rules" about how the world works based on what we experience. What rules about worth did you notice in yourself when answering these questions?

Systemic Wealth Inequality: What It Is and How It Fucks Us All

B efore we get into the brain science part, it's important for us to chat, at least a little bit, about the environment our brains exist in . . . which is one of *systemic wealth inequality*. You aren't going to feel like you are back in econ, I promise. Or at least, you will feel like you are in the punk rock version of econ where you actually get to understand why our economy is a post-apocalyptic shit show that is structured from the bottom up to fuck you over.

You have absolutely heard about wealth inequality, right? The short definition is that there is a big gap between the net worth (the financial kind, not the self-worth kind) of a relatively small number of rich people and the rest of us. That gap is growing in most countries.

Income inequality was the focus of the Occupy Wall Street movement, which started in the US in 2011. The point of Occupy was to highlight and change social and economic injustice and how the global financial system (and large corporations . . . which have more rights than my uterus at this point in time) benefit very few people. And how this arrangement is causing widespread instability and making the whole idea of democracy a sham. As the late Supreme Court Justice Louis Brandeis once said, *"We must make our choice. We may have democracy, or we may have wealth concentrated in the hands of a few, but we can't have both."*

This isn't a book on deconstructing capitalism as a form of system oppression. Those books have been written and there is no benefit to me re-writing them (plus I really don't need any new notes in my FBI file, I hear it's getting unwieldy). But understanding the insanity of the structure is still important, because we are all doing our own work around living in a broken system. If you're going to separate your net worth from your sense of self-worth, you must first understand what is and isn't in your control. You don't have to personally dismantle global capitalism to start a savings account!

Let's start with some basic terminology.

Wealth = Net worth

Net worth = assets minus liabilities

Assets are your money in the bank, anything you own that has value, like a house or car or massive collection of rare 7-inches, intellectual property from art you've created, or your own business, and the value of any investments you have, like stocks, bonds, retirement accounts.

Liabilities are the debts you owe.

And yes, there are absolutely a ton of people who have a negative net worth. This is why Chris Rock was dead right when he stated that, sure, Shaq may be *rich*, but the man who signs his checks has *wealth.* What would be a breathtaking amount of money for any of us (and was for Shaq), it was *nothing* to the individuals who have the type of assets that allow them to own a professional sports team and cover a payroll of *many* highly-paid individuals. And a good number of those highly-paid individuals may be living paycheck to paycheck for a multitude of reasons. Almost all of us are only a few bad months away from being thrown into poverty (if we are not there already). But none of us (reading this book anyway) are a few good months away from being billionaires.

To give you a snapshot of how income inequality has grown just in the few years since the Occupy Wall Street movement: In 2018, three men (Jeff Bezos, Bill Gates, and Warren Buffett) had a combined wealth that added up to more than the wealth of the least wealthy half of Americans. One percent of Americans own more than 50% of all stocks. The inequality in these numbers has spiked over the past few decades and now wealth inequality levels and income inequality levels in the United States have reached what they were before the great stock market crash of 1929, and are just as racialized.

(And as an aside, I wrote all of this in 2019, but as I go through edits before we go to press in June of 2020? Damn, I wish I had been wrong.)

This is pretty high on the list of shit that doesn't bode well. And the reason that doesn't bode well is not just that economic collapse could destroy our lives in ways that we can already imagine, but also because it's slowly killing us in ways that most of us haven't imagined. Wealth inequality fucks with our physical and mental health in a serious way. When we look at global data about wealth distribution and compare it with other data about health, we get some interesting results. It turns out that we can correlate mental health and physical health issues *not just to socio-economic status, but to wealth inequality overall.* We already know that poverty is correlated with worse outcomes in physical and mental health. But on top of that, in places with major income inequality, everyone's mental and physical health suffers, rich and poor.

Inequality operates as a *contextual stressor.* This means it isn't just one of the regular stressors of being human. It's something that has to be "overcome" by some of us, while for others it's never a concern. This divide creates social comparison (which is just how we rank ourselves in areas that are important to us in comparison with other people . . . and how we define our self-worth based on that ranking) and breaks down cohesion (which is, simply, our agreement to work together for a common goal). So this is fucking with our sense of self-worth through a false mechanism for judging the worth of those around us.

If rich people don't have this contextual stressor, why is it fucking them up too? For the same reason that dumping chemicals into the drinking water poisons everyone in the end. It's not ultimately containable. Negative physical health issues (including infant mortality rates) are higher. Rates of clinical depression and schizophrenia are higher. Even people who are winning at the wealth game are tethered into this contest that creates a level of stress in their bodies that causes real, physical damage.

This isn't an accident though. Society is *designed* to maintain a structure of poverty and inequality (and, therefore, social control). And I feel that it is important to highlight a few of these structural inequalities in order for us to recognize how systemic it really is. Stay with me for a moment while I get grouchy and political for a minute, using examples from the particularly fucked system that is the U.S.:

- If you are unable to work and therefore receive disability benefits, you cannot have more than $2000 of assets in the bank. So you can keep the Medicaid that provides the medical care that keeps you alive, but you can't squirrel away any money to start a small business or buy a piece of land to grow your own food.

- Under the Fair Labor Standards Act, it is legal to pay workers less than minimum wage if they have a disability that (theoretically) impacts their productivity. It is completely legal to pay someone less than a dollar an hour if the employer has gotten a certificate from the Wage and Labor Division. There are currently about a half a million people who are employed at subminimum wage, according to the department of labor. (Alaska recently implemented a new law that prevents disabled people from being paid less than minimum wage, so there are at least *some* instances of change in the right direction.)

- Prisoners are also paid subminimum wage for their labor. The Department of Justice Federal Prison Industries annual report in 2017 shows that prisoners make $0.23 to

$1.15 an hour, and in some states make nothing at all (like in Texas, where I live). So someone who does their time and is theoretically trying to reintegrate back into society has nothing to show for their labor while incarcerated. (As an added bonus, even for the individuals who are making that sweet $1.15 an hour, a $4 case of ramen noodles will cost them almost $17 from the prison commissary. If there is a way to steal back whatever was paid out, the prison system will find it.)

- Tipped workers make a subminimum wage. The subminimum wage used to be half of the federal minimum wage, but in 1996 it was decoupled from being calculated from the minimum wage. So when that increased to $7.25 an hour in 2009 (which is *still* not a livable wage), there was no increase for tipped workers, keeping it at $2.13. This system has led to workers being cheated out of millions of dollars in wages, according to the Department of Labor's own investigations. (Like the minimum wage, this varies from state to state—some states have a flat minimum wage, regardless of tips.)

- The criminalization of sex work and aggressive policing of such work has been a systemic way of disempowering individuals from accessing a career that allows independence, flexibility, and a living wage that lets them support themselves and their loved ones. (As George Carlin said, selling is legal and fucking is legal . . . so why isn't selling fucking legal?)

Obviously something has to change and fast. *And the place we start is in our own experience of ourselves in this system.* We can start by paying attention to the external system instead of our internal recrimination. We can start utilizing every fucking resource available to keep ourselves afloat, rather than feeling shame for needing them. If the airlines can get government bailouts, you can sure as fuck get a food pantry. And we can care for each other with a sense of unity and (yes) real cohesion.

When we feel frustrated for not getting ahead, it helps to remember that literally almost all of us are not getting ahead. When we feel like a failure at managing our money or debt, we need to remind ourselves that internalizing wealth inequality is creating a physical stress response that is literally making us sick while reinforcing the structure of a fucked up situation.

This is all to serve as a reminder that you are not broken. I would say the system is broken, but as just the few examples I listed above show, the system actually is working *just how it was designed to work.* And that's what needs changing.

Your Experiences Around Systemic Wealth Inequality

Some questions to explore and discuss:

- How were systemic wealth inequality and underpaid labor viewed as you were growing up? Were these issues you were made aware of? Educated on? How so?

- How are systemic wealth inequality and underpaid labor viewed and discussed within your current household? Friends and peers? How so?

- Have you noticed any tendencies in yourself to treat underpaid labor differently from appropriately compensated labor? How so? Do any particular circumstances make that difference more apparent (like for younger workers, etc.)?

- What is one immediate thing you can do that demonstrates a respect for the value of underpaid labor within your social circle?

- How can you create ongoing support for individuals providing underpaid labor within your social circle?

- How do you feel about the decriminalization of sex work industries? What concerns do you have? How have you seen sex work portrayed in media? How was it discussed when you were growing up? How is it discussed among your peer group?

How Poverty Perpetuates Trauma-Organized Systems

All these damn money books that aren't paying attention to the impact of trauma have been pissing me the fuck off. There is just no way we can talk about money without talking about trauma. I mean, if systemic wealth inequality is bad for *everyone*, what happens to those of us who experience poverty?

A short definition of trauma: It's a response created by your amygdala to try to protect you from re-experiencing difficult events. The amygdala is part of the limbic system, which is the part of the brain that connects and stories memories and emotions. Not the how-to-get-to-the-grocery-store memories, but the big life events memories. The amygdala's job is to keep you alive by assigning labels to certain events that have happened to you so it can help you stay safe in the future by remembering if a Big Life Event ended well or not.

If something happens that reminds you of a traumatic event, your amygdala hijacks your response system in an effort to protect you from being re-traumatized. So some location, or smell, or sensation, or *something* sends you right back to the traumatic event. When this happens you might start responding to your present life as if you are still in your past life, and still in your trauma experience of the previous Big Life Event—responding to your current surroundings as if you are *literally being retraumatized.*

This is not a bad thing in and of itself. If you trip on broken concrete and fall on your ass, that's the kind of thing you want to remember and watch out for in the future at an unconscious, automatic level. Especially if you walk down that sidewalk every day and the city isn't going to fix the problem anytime soon.

But the amygdala isn't going to discriminate . . . it's going to err on the side of caution, so we get a danger cue from all kinds of random pieces of the environment that don't actually pose a threat. Like if all sidewalk cracks get you turnt and you freeze in panic. When this happens again and again and you can't get out of it, that's a trauma response. Which oftentimes leads to post-traumatic stress disorder (PTSD).

For the record, that is what the word "trigger" actually means. It doesn't mean you are uncomfortable, it means you are reliving a traumatic event because a certain present day experience told your brain to go into fight-flight-freeze mode.

In urban, impoverished communities, there's a greater likelihood of exposure to multiple traumas and adverse life events. Up to 93% of individuals who grow up in urban poverty report trauma exposure (which is usually discovered when they end up in the justice system or community mental health system). This is because they are far more likely to be victims of or bear witness to crime and violence and are far more likely to experience abuse and neglect, just to name a couple of examples. Then add the simple fact that the continuous struggle of *not having enough fucking money* to provide for everyday needs is in-and-of-itself traumatic.

No matter where you live, when your daily life is crisis-informed, you are continuously triggered. This makes it hard not to operate from a place of chronic stress, toxic relationship strategies, and crisis-oriented coping strategies. In a nutshell, individuals living in poverty are far, far, far more likely to experience complex symptoms of traumatic distress, and that distress impacts the entirety of their family system in ways that mental health professionals and researchers didn't understand until the past few decades.

And it doesn't even take living in *chronic* poverty to develop a trauma reaction.

While studying financial personalities, research psychologist Galen Buckwalter kept bumping into something weird.

He was working with a "factor model" (a way to classify groups of personality traits) called HEXACO, which stands for honesty/humility, emotionality, extroversion, agreeableness, conscientiousness, openness. His hypothesis was that everyone would show some combination of these traits, either positively or negatively, in their attitudes about money. But in researching actual humans, Dr. Buckwalter kept finding traits that didn't fall into any of those categories. But these traits did align with how humans experience *fear*.

When unpacking the life circumstances of the individuals participating in his research, he found that those who presented with fear around money issues were experiencing the same kinds of symptoms he had seen when studying trauma and PTSD earlier in his career.

Yes, I know that "financial PTSD" doesn't actually exist as a diagnosis. And financial issues alone don't qualify anyone for a general PTSD diagnosis. But hang with me. Let's look at how PTSD is diagnosed:

- Intrusive thoughts (flashbacks, involuntary memories, stuck in anxious thinking patterns, upsetting dreams and nightmares).

- Avoiding reminders of the traumatic event (situations, people, places, activities, objects) and resisting talking about what happened and their feelings surrounding the event.

- Negative and often distorted thoughts and feelings about oneself or other people and/or feeling detached from others or from activities that used to be enjoyable.

- Arousal and reactive symptoms like irritability and anger, reckless or self-destructive behavior, struggles with sleeping or concentration. These symptoms are indicative of our body's *allostatic load,* which is defined by the International Encyclopedia of the Social & Behavioral Sciences, as *"the cost of chronic exposure to elevated or fluctuating endocrine or neural responses resulting from chronic or repeated challenges that the individual experiences as stressful"* which is just a fancy way of saying the body gets overwhelmed by trauma as much as the brain does.

Dr. Buckwalter went on to define *financial* PTSD as *"the physical, emotional, and cognitive deficits people experience when they cannot cope with either abrupt financial loss or the chronic stress of having inadequate financial resources."*

He has found that 23% of all adults (and 36% of millennials because society has fucked y'all over extra much) show symptoms of financial PTSD. And it only takes one of two things to happen. Either a big traumatic financial loss (losing a job, foreclosing a home, a shitty divorce settlement) or 3+ months of not having enough income to meet one's monthly expenses.

Now let's look at what Dr. Buckwalter found in the people who were demonstrating financial PTSD:

- Rumination on financial failure

- Negative thought processes about money in general

- Perseveration about financial doom

- Seeing the world as fundamentally hostile and that it's only a matter of time before shit's fucked again

- Avoidance of the mail, phone calls, etc. (because, bill collectors)

- Allostatic load is over the top. People are jittery, not sleeping well, have nightmares

- Little experience of joy and meaning

- Increase in unhealthy coping mechanisms like substance use or other avoidance strategies

- Isolation from others (especially if their financial PTSD was related to coercive control)

And there we go. That fits, doesn't it? Like a damn glove. So even if it isn't diagnosable, it is reality.

The hard part is, recovering from financial PTSD means not just getting a better handle on your finances, it means dealing with the intrusive thoughts, arousal, avoidance, and negative cognitions that you are experiencing in regards to your money. When your body and mind are just completely depleted, doing all the financial literacy shit you are supposed to be doing is almost impossible . . . you just don't have the emotional and intellectual space for it.

Even if you do somehow find the emotional and intellectual bandwidth for it, you are then faced with the misguided concept that financial health is achieved through being an overly-regimented, no-fun-having, money saving machine. That *also* feels miserable and overwhelming, even if we do dredge up enough energy to start lining up our ducks . . . so we generally fail. (Which is why, later on in this book, we are gonna figure out what financial health looks like for *you*, not for an investment broker.)

Back in the 90s, a British psychoanalyst named Arnon Bentovin coined the term *trauma-organized system*, which refers to the way that a social system (like a family living in poverty) becomes fundamentally and unconsciously organized around the chronic toxicity they are experiencing. *They make decisions from this place of fear and traumatic stress, even when those decisions are a detriment to themselves and others within the family.* They are continuously trauma reactive, in the ways I wrote more about in my book *Unfuck Your Brain*.

We understand that someone who has experienced sexual violence may shut down physically, even when they are with a loving partner and want to be able to connect physically, right? People living under the continuous stress of poverty experience the same kind of shutdown in relation to managing money and finances, even when they have enough money to live comfortably in the present.

Financial crisis or long-term poverty creates a kind of trauma residue that carries forward into our lives, even when no longer poor. Take my friend's experience as an example:

> *I was really dumb about money and making future goals until my 30s. Even after my mom married my stepdad and we were no longer poor, my whole family seemed to operate in continuous crisis with him now along for the ride. Even though I moved out when I was 20, I was reacting to life as if I was still in that family system. There were plenty of people around me that modeled blowing whatever extra cash you had on partying, because why not? I drank a lot and did a lot of drugs, even after I had a career-trajectory*

job. It didn't occur to me to save or even to buy a house.
Apartments were easier to get out of. And felt temporary by
nature. At some level, I really expected to die young, so why
think about the future?

Maybe there is something in my friend's experience you can relate
to, and you are realizing that some of your attitudes and behaviors
around money are a product of your earlier life experiences.
Recognizing what's going on is the biggest part of creating change,
right? Once we are able to start saying, *"Oops, there's my bullshit,"*
we have a different relationship with it.

This is the part of the book where I tell you that therapy doesn't
have to suck and doesn't mean you're fucked up. And seeing a
therapist to focus on your financially activated trauma reactions is
a good, good, good idea.

So the first activity I have here is designed to help you unpack how
financial stress has caused trauma reactions for you. It's something
you can share with a therapist (ahem) so you have a focus for your
work . . . and/or use it when doing your independent self-healing.

And since I am all for self-healing, with or without the assistance
of a therapist, I'm including a couple of exercises that I designed
specifically to help you manage the activation that occurs when
your financial PTSD starts taking you over.

Financial Trauma Symptoms

What symptoms have you experienced due to poverty, financial stress, or financial overwhelment within the following categories?

Intrusive thoughts (flashbacks, involuntary memories, stuck in anxious thinking patterns, upsetting dreams and nightmares).

In the past:

Currently:

Avoiding reminders of the traumatic event (situations, people, places, activities, objects) and resisting talking about what happened and their feelings surrounding the event.

In the past:

Currently:

Negative and often distorted thoughts and feelings about oneself or other people and/or feeling detached from others or activities that used to be enjoyable.

In the past:

Currently:

Arousal and reactive symptoms like irritability and anger, reckless or self-destructive behavior, struggles with sleeping or concentration—your body gets overwhelmed by trauma as much as your brain does.

In the past:

Currently:

Financial Fear Mindfulness Practice

When you find yourself stuck and overwhelmed by financial fears, try feeling it without letting it take over. Our thoughts and feelings change the minute we start paying attention to them in a mindful way. It's like examining something under a microscope . . . the minute you turn on the light so you can see better, whatever you are looking at starts to react to the light, changing what you see.

1) **Experience the present.**

   What's going on right now? What are you thinking? Feeling? What's going on in your body?

2) **Take a deeper dive.**

   Where are these feelings in your body? How big or small? How strong or weak? The thoughts you are experiencing, how do they sound?

3) **Take off the judgy-pants.**

   Just notice all of these experiences (thoughts, feelings, somatic responses) as something you have. Not something you are. Make yourself a judgement-free zone. They are not good or bad, they are just information from your body in the present moment that are activated by your experiences of financial fear. Right now we aren't worried about fixing anything, just listening to ourselves.

4) Practice self-compassion.

Think of someone you love. A friend, a family member. Someone who is fundamentally a good person who has made mistakes but always gets back up and tries their best. What would you tell that person if they were going through this experience. Got an idea? Cool. Now tell *yourself* that.

Test Your Financial Thinking

Trauma reactions often lead to us framing everything in a negative light. We start to expect that everything will be fucked all the time. Cognitive behavioral therapy is super helpful in framing how to unpack and challenge that constant negativity. This is a classic CBT skill framed specifically for financial PTSD.

- What's the financial situation that you are focused on right now?

- What are you thinking or imagining is happening or going to happen?

- What emotions are you experiencing?

- What bodily sensations?

- What makes me think that my thoughts are true? Any evidence?

- What makes me think my thoughts are not true (or not completely true)? Any evidence?

- What's another way you can look at this situation that's more helpful?

- What's the worst thing that can happen?

- What could you do then?

- What's the ideal outcome?

- What would you do then?

- What's the most probable outcome?

- What can you do then?

- What might be different if I change my thinking?

- If I was giving advice to a friend going through this same thing, what would I tell them?

VRRR

The Conflation of Money and Labor

nother thing that can really fuck up our sense of worth under capitalism is our relationship with and expectations around unpaid labor.

Unpaid labor refers simply to any work that does not receive direct remuneration. When we think of unpaid labor, we generally think of household chores, errands, and the care of other human beings in the household (childcare, eldercare, and the care of individuals with disabilities). But it also includes other things that all fall under the category of *"productive activities"* which includes things like growing our own food, collecting or hunting for food, making or mending clothes, fixing household items, collecting fuel or water, or any of the myriad of ways human beings sustained their lives and the lives of their families and larger cultural group before money existed.

The bulk of unpaid labor across the globe is done by women. And while that gap is closing (hey, thank you millenials!), we have a ways to go before there is no longer, you know, a *gap*. Partially because some unpaid labor like pregnancy, childbirth, and breastfeeding/chestfeeding is by default the domain of women, outside of a small but growing group of badass trans men and nonbinary individuals. But mostly the gap exists because the industrial revolution created different categories of contribution. Industry paid money. Everything else fell under the umbrella of *domestic duties*. So even now, when most women are doing an equal amount of paid labor in the workforce, they are still doing more unpaid labor when they get home, compared to their male counterparts.

Even in relationships where one person is working in the labor market, and one person is engaging in "domestic" labor, there is a dual dependency between these individuals. The individual engaging in the paid labor is dependent on the work of the individual doing the unpaid labor, not just vice-versa.

Could you just imagine if a country's economic output included unpaid labor? A study in 2010 found that if unpaid work was incorporated in measuring the gross domestic product of the US, it would have raised the GDP by 26%. That is a *ton* of work that we are not accounting for when we look at how societies run. And if we aren't accounting for it, we aren't valuing it or honoring it.

There are plenty of policy suggestions out there that would create fundamental changes in how domestic labor is respected, accounted for, and reimbursed. In the meantime, part of unfucking our worth is noticing these patterns in our own lives and finding places we can challenge the status quo.

Maybe you do a lot of unpaid labor—or none of your labor is paid. This isn't necessarily a bad thing. Maybe you whole-heartedly and joyfully chose to be a stay-at-home caretaker. But this can impact your financial freedom in a multitude of ways, such as your ability to establish your own credit or make independent decisions.

Or maybe you benefit from the unpaid labor of others, whether or not you are paid for your efforts in the world. I mean, I think we all have at some point. But if we aren't recognizing and valuing this labor, we are contributing to the lessening of the worth of those who are providing it.

This isn't intellectual exercise bullshit. It all ties back into the system that continues to devalue our self-worth and our collective appreciation of the slew of ways we contribute to society. And that becomes the fertilizer for growing a nice, green field of financial trauma.

Your Experiences Around Unpaid Labor

- How were paid and unpaid labor viewed when you were growing up? Were they centered and respected differently? How so?

- How is paid and unpaid labor viewed and discussed within your current household? Friends and peers? Are they centered and respected differently? How so?

- Have you noticed any tendencies in yourself to treat unpaid labor differently from paid labor? How so? Any particular circumstances that make it more likely?

- What is one immediate thing you can do that demonstrates a respect for the value of unpaid labor within your social circle?

- How can you create ongoing support for unpaid labor within your social circle?

Coercive Financial Control

C oercive control is a non-physical form of abuse that occurs through systematic boundary violation. I'm talking about it at this point in the book because it happens when there are power imbalances, and because it's a form of financial PTSD that doesn't get talked about enough. But putting it here in the context of talking about systemic poverty doesn't mean it's caused by poverty. It's caused by people being assholes.

First off, it does need to be said that someone setting limits and boundaries around the money they give or lend to you isn't necessarily coercive control. Back when I was in high school, my uncle offered to help pay for my college if I was interested in studying oenology. He was hoping I would run a vineyard with him and clearly stated the boundaries and limits of the money up front. It was by no means coercive control on his part to then not help pay for my psychology degree instead.

Coercive control is a tool of emotional terrorism designed to illict fear-based compliance in another person. Coercive control exists within all manner of intimate relationships, in LGBTQ+

communities, among family members, within friendship groups, and within employer-employee relationships. The common denominator of unequal status applies to the dynamic of controller and controlled. Those with less power are far more susceptible to oppressive behavior by others whom they rely on for food, shelter, financial support, and/or safety. These behaviors are almost always legal, so they continue to happen.

You don't have to ever have been physically hurt to have been abused. Individuals who were victims of coercive control show the same trauma responses as individuals who have been physically abused. The research on coercive control shows that the loss of autonomy leads to PTSD far more than physical injury. And financial abuse fucks up relationships even more than other experiences of financial PTSD.

If you recognize these patterns in one of your relationships, do know that there is support for getting out of an abusive situation. Even if the person abusing you has never hurt you physically, domestic violence agencies can help you strategize a plan to leave safely (or stay safely, if that is currently your best option).

The most obvious indicator of financial abuse is the direct control of household resources, such as:

- Bank accounts being managed by only one person, with the other person being either given an allowance, brought shopping, or having to ask for money for any purchases, no matter who is producing the income

- Major decisions about family income being made by only one person

- All assets being in the name of and/or controlled by one person (mortgage, rental agreement, cars, etc.)

But it can also look like the control of other aspects of your life that impact your financial autonomy, such as:

- Controlling access to medical care

- Controlling the use of contraceptives or STI prevention methods

- Interfering with or threatening your immigration/citizenship status

- Creating other legal trouble for you

- Threatening your housing stability (e.g., threatening to kick you out of a home they pay for, breaking rules set in a home rental to have your lease terminated and get you both evicted)

- Keeping you from work/making you late to work/disrupting your workday/getting you fired

- Destroying your property

- Destroying the property of your friends and family

- Anything else that causes you a level of financial strain that you cannot afford

If this is something you experienced in the past, it's important to realize how coercive control of finances is a form of abuse and the fact that you are an abuse survivor may be playing a role in your present relationships and finances.

If it's something you are dealing with in the present, I hope you approach your situation like you would any other abusive situation and find ways to be safe, whether you plan to leave or decide to stay.

Does "Happiness" Matter Here?

There was a study conducted back in the '70s which has been passed around like a cultural meme in the decades since. The researchers found that individuals who won the lottery were not significantly happier than their control group counterparts . . . nor were a group of individuals with spinal cord injuries particularly sadder than the same control group counterparts. The study authors postulated that human beings have a *happiness set point.* Meaning that after a big life event (positive or negative) we return to a specific level of happiness that is just inherent to our personality.

This research had always made me grumpy in my little radical activist heart. It seems like the kind of thing that society tells poor people in order to put their problems back on their shoulders, rather than doing something as a community to raise everyone's quality of life, right? Like *"Giving you healthcare really won't make you any happier, we've found. So you just keep working hard and maybe you will achieve your goals . . . and in the meantime be grateful for all you have!"*

More recent research has parsed out more detailed information about the influence of life events on our quality of life. It turns out that financial gains *do* make us happier. People who win the lottery (or experience other positive life events that have nothing to do with money, like having a family, and, yes, even finalizing a divorce after a difficult separation) consistently report an improvement in their mental health, and those improvements stay stable over time. A financial uptick in our lives allows us access to resources. We can get caught up on our bills, afford to go to the dentist, take care of the family member who took care of us, etc. The money itself doesn't make us happier, but the money as a form of energy to make our lives better matters.

The idea of a happiness set point isn't total crap (most research isn't *total* crap, we just tend to oversimplify it rather than look at the bigger picture). Some people have all the money in the world and they are still grumpy fucks, right?

I mean, think of it this way. When our self-worth is tied to our finances, we are far more likely to experience negative psychological outcomes like anxiety and depression. It also fucks with our sense of autonomy, which makes it harder to bounce back from financial stressors. Researchers at the University of Buffalo found this to be true, even when controlling for participants' actual financial status. Meaning, *it didn't matter how much they had* . . . if their worth was centered around money, they were messed up about money.

Poor kids may have more trauma exposure, but rich kids are more likely to suffer from anxiety, depression, substance use and abuse, eating disorders, cheating, and stealing. Wealthy adults, similarly, have higher rates of depression and less relationship satisfaction.

Money is often used to hide problems, rather than as a resource to access fixing them.

And, hey . . . maybe all this trauma/poverty stuff doesn't apply to you. Maybe you grew up pretty financially comfortable but realize you still have a weird and unhealthy relationship with money and wealth that you want to get over. And this gets back to systemic wealth inequality being bad for *all* of us.

Some years ago, a 16 year old boy in Texas sat trial for killing four people while driving drunk. He got off with ten years probation, in yet another instance where I find myself apologizing for my fucking state.

During the trial, the term *affluenza* was used by an expert witness (a psychologist named G. Dick Miller) to explain why the teen was likely unaware of how his behaviors could negatively impact others. Affluenza is a fairly recent term coined to describe the unhealthy psychological and social effects that affluence can have on individuals. It can create feelings of guilt, social isolation, and a lack of motivation for personal growth and achievement.

Dr. G. Dick later said he regretted using the term on the stand but it raised some really interesting dialogue in the media surrounding the trial about *the rich and the rest of us* (to borrow the phrasing of Dr. Cornel West and Tavis Smiley). If too little money is a considerable problem, what about too much?

Research continues to show that people who have money (especially like a lot a lot of money) are far more likely to subscribe to the idea of class essentialism, which is a subset of social Darwinism.

Essentialism just means the belief that differences between any two groups of people are due to fundamental, inborn differences in the people themselves. *Race essentialism* holds that people of color simply commit more crimes than white people and therefore should be arrested in greater numbers and be more at risk of police brutality. Which we all know is fucking ridiculous. (I mean, we all do know that, right? We don't have to have that convo today, do we?)

Class essentialism says the same thing about money. Class essentialists think that if you have more money than everyone else it's because you fucking worked harder than anyone else, are smarter than anyone else, and are more deserving of this money than anyone else. Poor people know how hard they are working for what they have, so they don't typically believe this mythology, but research shows that rich people generally do.

If you believe in class essentialism, research suggests that you are not going to be down for social movements like restorative justice, either. If you are a class essentialist, why would you want to help others when you don't see them as doing the work they need to do to help themselves? Class essentialism becomes poisonous to *all* of society, not just the people that suffer from it.

This brings us back to the happiness set point. People that are stupid-rich aren't happier because of it. There is a sweet spot of having enough money to pay your bills, go to the doctor when you're sick, and go out for sushi every once in a while. But once you get up into the *"I dunno, should each of the maltipoos get their own Lear jet or is one enough for all of them?"* or even just the comfy six-figure income range, shit starts to fall apart.

Happiness isn't intrinsically tied to wealth— but what we think of as "happiness" *is* one of the signifiers of an overall positive mindset in cognitions and mood. And that's something we have more control over that we may think.

And that is where positive psychology comes into play. I've written about positive psychology as a tool in the past (*Unfuck Your Brain*, Microcosm 2017 to be exact). Martin Seligman is the daddy-o of the field, and he found that there are three traits to optimism that can actually be learned. They are permanence, pervasiveness, and personalization.

- Optimistic people don't see negative events as **permanent,** but instead frame them as temporary setbacks to be overcome.

- Optimistic people don't see failure in their lives as **pervasive . . .** meaning they don't see failing at one thing as being a failure at all the things.

- Optimistic people don't take shit **personally.** They see failures as events in their lives not as evidence of their lack of worth.

See how this could make a huge difference in how you view your worth as a human being outside of your financial wins or losses? The idea that we can make practical shifts in how we relate to the world in order to have a more positive outlook can help us deal with the bullshit we have on hand, which will bump our happiness set point up a notch and give us good tools for better mental health in general (even if we continue to not win the lottery).

Better tools in general are important to our ability to counteract our trauma-reactive behavior around money and our worth and value as human beings. And that's the opposite of swallowing capitalistic bullshit, right? So of course I included an easy, evidence-based learned optimism exercise to get you started.

Signs of Affluenza

1. What messages have you received about money equalling worth and value in society? Where did these messages come from?

2. Have you ever felt less-than because you had a lower salary, less money in the bank, couldn't afford to own expensive items?

3. Have you ever felt a sense of superiority over others because of what you had or could afford to have?

4. Have you ever used the money you had to prop up your ego or self-esteem?

5. Have you ever made decisions about money or earning money that were based on the pursuit of money for its own sake?

6. How are finances discussed in your family/social circle? Are purchases bragged about? Payoffs discussed as a cost of making life easier?

7. What brings value and meaning to your life that is not directly influenced by money?

Your Best Possible Future Self

This exercise was developed by Laura King and has been found to be incredibly effective in multiple controlled studies. It's super easy.

> Stop reading this. Close your eyes. Spend a few minutes imagining your best possible self ten years from now. Don't worry about the details of getting there. Just what your best possible future will be like. You can write it down if you want, but you don't have to. You can visualize it, or tell yourself the story, or . . .

Research shows that if you spend 20 minutes a day for four days on this exercise it does amazing things for your optimism about life. So do the thing. Four days in a row. And not just to bump your happiness set point, but because it is gonna be useful later in the book

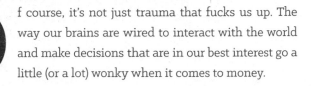

This is Your Brain on Money

O f course, it's not just trauma that fucks us up. The way our brains are wired to interact with the world and make decisions that are in our best interest go a little (or a lot) wonky when it comes to money.

Not because we are shitty human beings who have zero chill when there is money in our pockets, but because the strategies that made sense for human survival before industrialization don't make the same sense in modern society. And if we aren't aware that's what's going on, we are really likely to do stupid shit.

In this chapter, I'll talk about two of the biggest brain traps that can create problems for us around money. We know about these brain traps from the field of *behavioral economics*, which is focused on how we think and subsequently behave (duh) about money.

There are certain financial thought patterns that are so pervasive in our society that they impact almost everyone. Advertising execs prey on this shit. And even seasoned investors fall into these traps. Even financial guru types who move money around for a living get burned by these habits of mind. So if you recognize these traps in your own day-to-day interactions, know you are in good company.

And from here on out you will be better able to pay attention to them so you are able to outsmart them.

THE MENTAL ACCOUNTING TRAP

One of the biggest hurdles in being better with our finances is something called *mental accounting*. The term was introduced in 1999 by a professor of economics named Richard Thayer. He defined mental accounting as "the set of cognitive operations used by individuals and households to organize, evaluate, and keep track of financial activities." The term refers to how we treat money differently based on criteria we assign it. This affects how we spend money, and even how we invest it (if we are lucky enough to be able to do so).

Creating and organizing categories is a human brain 101 type exercise, but it doesn't work fantastically when it comes to something like money. Ultimately, money isn't real—it's a made-up system that works because we all agree it works. Its value isn't tied to anything concrete, like how much you work or even the availability of a precious metal, and it constantly shifts because of things like interest. Saving is not as simple as preserving some food for the cold winter months and eating the rest of it now, which is more what our brain was built for, so when faced with modern financial realities it gets super confused.

Mental accounting sounds complicated, but it's actually a pretty simple concept. It means we naturally assign all the money we have, expect, or plan to spend into different mental buckets. The problem is that our brains aren't very good at seeing the big picture.

We might have a mental account for groceries and one for clothes. That's not a problem until we run out of grocery money for the month and stop buying food (and get hungry) instead of curtailing our planned spending on clothes.

Or say someone gives us fifty dollars as a birthday gift. Or we get our tax refund or some other unexpected small windfall of awesomeness. We generally don't treat that money the same as the money we get in our paychecks or otherwise "earn." We interact with it differently and treat it like a different form of energy. So instead of putting it towards our new washing machine or buying books for school, which we were already worried our regular paycheck wouldn't cover, we treat ourselves to something fabulous that may not be in line with our goals.

Another example shows how we treat materially identical purchases differently. In 1984, someone did a study where people were given one of two scenarios. In the first scenario, you were going to the movies and had pre-purchased your ticket. Ten bucks. But when you got there you realized that you had lost your ticket (because in 1984 you couldn't just pull it up on your phone, right?). The question was: do you buy a new ticket? 46% of the people said "yeah, I'd replace the ticket." Less than half of them.

Second scenario in the study: you're going to the movie and you haven't bought your ticket yet. When you go to buy it you realize that you have ten dollars less in your wallet than you thought you did (whomp-whomp). When the researchers asked if they would still buy the ticket, 88% of the study participants said they would. In both cases, individuals are getting information that says *"this movie is going to cost you twenty dollars instead of ten . . . and you are ten down no matter what."* But the mental accounting of that first ten dollars going bye-bye is different enough to the human brain that it affected their decision about the movie.

Mental accounting takes into account the psychology of choice. Meaning our rules about money are not neutral, and are affected by the attractiveness and desirability of our options. What Richard Thayer (who won the Nobel Prize in 2017 for this work, so we should listen to the man) is saying is a dollar is a dollar is a dollar. No matter what category we put it in or where it came from. It's *fungible*. Its worth doesn't change. Its energy doesn't change. And that's a thought we need to hold on to when making financial decisions so our decisions are more conscious.

Your Mental Accounting Experiences
Reflect on these questions, or have a discussion:

- How have you treated different sources of money differently in the past?

- Have you made any financial decisions based on mental accounting that you regretted later?

THE SOCIAL INFLUENCE TRAP
We are influenced by others all the time, generally without even recognizing it. Did you know that just showing people a picture of a library will make them start speaking more quietly? And research has shown time and again that our feelings about policy changes

are more influenced by our feelings about the political party behind the suggested policy, rather than the policy itself (I am so guilty of this, it isn't the least bit cute).

We like to think that we are in charge of our decision-making, but the reality is our subconscious is sifting through all kinds of information on a continuous basis, and a trillion little decisions are being made at this level. The urge to imitate others is built into our nature. It makes evolutionary sense (if other people are running from lions you are gonna run, too) and is integral to our development (imitation is literally how we learn to talk, right?).

Social influence can be negative as well as positive. True (and hugely funny) story. The clothing brand Ambercrombie and Fitch offered to pay the cast of Jersey Shore to *not* wear their clothes on the show. They didn't want the brand associated with Snookie and friends.

The fact that we are hardwired to imitate and belong absolutely affects how we interact with money. As with all other forms of brain dumb-assery the answer lies in awareness: making these processes conscious. This means looking at how our family of origin interacted with money. And how the people who surround us now interact with money. Our friends, housemates, romantic partners, co-workers.

And not even just the people that we spend physical time with, but the people we connect with through the media. A recent survey done by Ally Bank found that 74% of millenials noted that social media influenced their shopping. And that isn't to say *"ugh, millennials."* Even those of us who aren't all up on insta are still being influenced by some sort of media. By the magazines we read, the TV we watch, whatever.

By making an effort to become aware of the social influences that affect our money habits and beliefs, we can better examine our decision making processes and decide if they serve us or not.

What Are Your Social Influences?

Think about the people that raised you or otherwise greatly influenced you growing up. Your parents, siblings, other family members. Guardians. Teachers. Friends and family of friends. You know, the whole village. Reflect on:

- What interactions did you have around your allowance, if you had one

- What about interactions around other money you were given (birthday money, babysitting money, etc.)

- What discussions about money do you remember?

- Fights about money?

- What financial topics were *not* talked about?

- What things do you remember wanting that cost money? Did you get them?

- What other things were purchased for you? Who made those decisions? What influenced those decisions?

- What is your most positive childhood memory about money or how money was used (to buy something, do something, etc?)

- What is your most negative?

- Anything that you noticed in these answers that surprised you? Or that you think might be an important influence on your relationship with money now?

Ok, ow. As much fun as that was, now we are gonna do it again with your life now. Think about your current family. Whether you are still embedded with your biological family or have one of your own. Think about your partners, past and present. Your closest friends. Your coworkers. The people you interact with on the regular.

- What are your interactions about your income?

- What about your interactions around other money you have/get (from family, partners, etc.)?

- What discussions about money do you have?

- What fights?

- What money-related things are *not* talked about?

- What things did you want in the recent past or want now that cost money? Did you or will you get them?

- What kinds of things are purchased for you? Who made those decisions? What influenced those decisions?

- What is your most positive adult memory about money or how money was used (to buy something, do something, etc.)?

- What is your most negative?

- Anything that you noticed in these answers that surprised you? Or that you realize has more influence on your life than you thought?

Money and Addiction

One other thing we really need to talk about for a minute when discussing how our worth gets fucked up? Addiction stuff. Specifically, addiction stuff that has a direct money tie-in. That is, the things that are considered addictions that directly involve money (versus things that are addictive that just *cost* money). The two biggies? Shopping and gambling. Which, interestingly, each affects the brain in completely different ways.

Shopping addiction? Is that a real thing?

Do you buy way too much dumb shit? Or maybe it's cool shit, but in amounts that are kind of embarrassing (says the person who owns every grey sweater ever manufactured in her size). Are you worried that your shopping may be a problem?

Sure, it could be . . . but maybe not in the way that you think.

Because first off, there is no such thing as a shopping addiction. I am saying all this not to dismiss or discount problematic shopping behaviors, but to make sure they are understood properly. I tend to get yelly when I see issues being oversimplified. And when it comes to mental health issues, that tendency to dumb shit down is what sets people up for failure to recover from them. And I know I don't have any dumb people reading my books. I got so many notes from y'all thanking me for the level of detail I spend explaining neuroscience in my books.

So second off, when you see the term shopping addiction, I want you to replace it in your own prefrontal cortex with the term *compulsive buying disorder.* And yes, that means the acronym is CBD, I also snort out-loud at this.

Shopping addiction is a phrase that hasn't *ever* existed in the Diagnostic and Statistical Manual of Mental Disorders (the DSM, the fancy book clinicians use to assign diagnosis). At the time of this writing, we are using the DSM V, which was published in 2013. An older version of the DSM, the DSM III (which was used from 1980 to 1994) *did* include compulsive buying disorder as an example of an *impulse control disorder, not otherwise specified,* though that particular term went bye-bye in the DSM-IV.

Meaning even back when I was riding my dinosaur to my undergrad psych classes in 1992 we still didn't think of shopping as an *addiction,* but as a symptom of other shit going on in a person's life. CBD generally runs in families, and exists with another diagnosis, like mood disorders, anxiety disorders, eating disorders, and other impulse disorders.

Survey-based research shows that about 6%-16% of any first-world population would qualify as compulsive buyers. These same surveys also demonstrate that 80%-95% of individuals who qualify as having a CBD are women, though that's likely a survey design problem. Interestingly, most research reviews on CBD have noted the same thing that I have noticed in my practice . . . that men are far more likely to call themselves "collectors" or use any other word than "shopper." So if you find that while you don't have a compulsive buying disorder, you *do* over-collect grey sweaters (ahem), this may still apply to you.

CBD patterns have been studied, and people who engage in the behavior generally report feeling negative emotions (anger, depression, anxiety, self-criticism, boredom) that are alleviated when they make a new purchase. The overlap varies from study to study, but one study I read showed that literally 100% of the people with CBD also had a mood disorder.

Shopping can provide a feeling of relief from the fuckitude of the other stuff people are feeling. *It gives us a sense of control when we feel out of control.*

So it makes sense that there isn't a generalized pattern of CBD development and treatment. Managing CBD happens when we manage the underlying fuckitude. There are studies that show treating depression in people with CBD also causes remission of CBD. Using cognitive behavior therapy techniques to identify and manage the negative thoughts that activate the shopping impulse has been shown to be effective for the same reason.

When we can recognize "I feel like shit and utterly powerless" and work with those thoughts and feelings, we are far less likely to medicate them with impulsive behavior. Whether that behavior is texting selfies to an ex for attention, vaguebooking continuously, picking fights with friends, *or buying our 7th pair of black boots that we absolutely do not need* (except for the fact that they go great with the grey sweaters!).

A lot of other people have found that they better manage their shopping habits through self-help books (hey, we got that one down!), and/or joining groups that focus on simplicity, sustainability, and minimalism. Marie Kondo and her focus on only keeping things in your life that spark joy is all in for that one.

Is Your Shopping a Problem?

Consider these questions:

- Do you prefer to shop alone?

- Do you shop to avoid uncomfortable or painful feelings?

- Do you feel better when you purchase something and then guilty later?

- Do you buy a lot of stuff you don't need and/or end up never using?

- Do you hide what you are buying from others?

- Do you lie (outright or by omission) about your purchases or the cost of them?

- Is your shopping causing financial problems for you (even if just diverting from your other financial goals)?

If these questions are ringing any bells for you, a lot of the budgeting tools that you will find later in the book and in the workbook can be really helpful if you are trying to de-grey-sweater your life. The austerity month challenge in particular can be a really good habit disruptor.

But any of these exercises should go along with *treatment for the underlying issues you are struggling with*. Remember that compulsive buying is a symptom of other stuff going on, and you deserve real healing.

Gambing addiction, definitely a real thing

Gambling is the other big money-based problem that a lot of people struggle with and you may be trying to figure out if this relates at all to your life.

When we think of gambling, we think of the traditional methods. Like playing poker or betting on the ponies. However, technology is creating new ways for our un-modern brains to get hooked in, and it also makes sense to consider (and start researching) how some things that seem to fall under the "shopping" category may be lighting us up in a way similar to other gambling behaviors. The European Union started stricter regulations around gaming loot boxes and the like for just this reason. If the behavior has a risk/ reward ratio that is different than simply spending too much at the mall, we need to take into consideration that this might be an issue.

Gambling is *way* different from compulsive buying in how it relates to the brain and mental health. Remember all the blahblahDSMblah I mentioned above? The story is entirely different when we are talking about gambling addiction. Historically, gambling disorders were classified much like CBD—as an impulse-control disorder. But the current DSM (DSM V) moved gambling to the section on substance-related and addictive disorders.

Gambling Disorder is literally the only non-substance related addiction in the DSM. I'm going over all this because, once again, y'all are smart as hell and don't need info dumbed down even a little bit in order to understand it. And when we understand shit, we can deal with it in an actually effective way.

We can see the difference in the brain of someone who has taken drugs right? It's "lit up" in a way that is different from someone raw-dogging life. A fuck-ton of research shows that gambling behaviors function like a substance addiction, whereas shopping behaviors simply do not light up the brain in the same way. While shopping behaviors are efficaciously treated with the same protocols that are used to treat mood disorders (like antidepressants and CBT), individuals that are addicted to gambling don't respond to those treatments.

You know what *does* help with gambling addiction? Opioid antagonists like naltrexone, which block the brain's ability to create all the dopamine that gets the craving cycle activated again.

Other effective supports include addictions-based counseling and 12-step programs (Gamblers Anonymous has been around since the 50s, only 20 years after Alcoholics Anonymous was started). And just like in the substance recovery world, Buddhist-Derived Interventions (BDIs) like Refuge Recovery are being used for gambling addictions just as they have been for drug and alcohol dependence.

The recidivism rate for gambling addiction is really high (about 75% . . . and that's with the understanding that only about 20% of people who have a gambling addiction seek treatment to begin with). That is likely a function of the fact that the people who experienced a relapse weren't being treated effectively. So if this is you, or someone you love, or a client you are working with? Fight for the real, efficacious, addictions-based treatments that reflect what's really going on in the brain.

Do You Have a Gambling Addiction?

Circle the numbers of the statements that have applied to you in the last year. If you're finding it difficult to answer honestly, remember your COAL from the beginning of the book.

1. You are spending more and more money when gambling in order to achieve the same excitement as before.

2. When you have tried to stop gambling or decrease your gambling, you have become restless and irritable.

3. When you have tried to stop gambling or decrease your gambling, you have been repeatedly unsuccessful.

4. You think about gambling frequently, such as planning your next gambling experience and mentally revisiting previous experiences, and you are focused on ways of getting money so you can gamble again.

5. When you don't feel well emotionally, you are far more likely to gamble.

6. If you lose money gambling, you want to gamble more in order to even out your losses ("chasing" one's losses).

7. You have had to rely on others to help with gambling related money problems

8. You have lied to conceal your gambling activities.

9. Your gambling has significantly affected another life domain in a negative way, such as losing or jeopardizing a relationship, a job, or an educational opportunity.

Gambling addiction can be formally diagnosed if you have experienced at least four of these issues in the past year. If this resonates with you, finding a therapist who specializes in this treatment or a peer recovery group may be helpful to your recovery.

Gambling Addiction Treatment Resources

SAMHSA's National Helpline
A confidential, free, 24-hour-a-day, 365-day-a-year, information service, in English and Spanish
1-800-662-HELP (4357)
TTY: 1-800-487-4889

Gamblers Anonymous
12 step abstinence model for gambling addiction
GamblersAnonymous.org

Gam-Anon International Service

Another 12 step abstinence based model

Gam-Anon.org

Smart Recovery

A 12-step alternative based in cognitive behavioral therapy, Smart Recovery does address gambling addiction, not just substance addiction.

SmartRecovery.org/gambling-addiction/

CONCLUSION

I mean, I could go on and on and do a whole encyclopedia set of books about the brain and how it's quirks of assholery cause us so many financial problems. But I think we all got the picture now, right? This is the most important shit. And any of the smaller pieces that have come into play in your own life make a lot more sense.

Because now you have some Official Brain Science(™) to use when you are trying to figure out your money and worth shit. Yes, there are a ton of "financial gurus" (gross term) out there saying bullshittery like *"You just have zero self control and suck as a human being."*

But you don't need to internalize their bullshittery anymore (thank Buddha, because fuck them all in the ear).

Now you counter those messages with *"Wait a minute, do I suck as a human being or is this a brain quirk that I need to pay attention to?"*

In case you're wondering, here's the answer to that question:

> *You aren't failing as a human being. It is a brain quirk that you need to pay attention to. Paying attention creates the space that allows for real change.*

And the next section of this book are the tools for the real change. Helping you figure out what is important to *you* about money, value, and worth so you can make decisions that come from that space instead of from what other people have been feeding you.

And it ain't easy. You may have been struggling with some financial PTSD for some time and avoiding all of this tough work for exactly that reason. Or dealing with the dichotomy of trying to live by other people's values instead of your own. Or fighting internalized messages about money being a measure of your worth in society. Or struggling with an addiction or compulsive behavior as a result of other mental health stuff. All those things will fuck a person up.

But now you know how to call bullshit. Which gives you the capacity to say *"That's just my brain lying to me in my own voice"* and then use tools to manage the feelings of activation and keep working through it. This is how we do the hard things.

PART TWO

UNFUCK YOUR WORTH

I f there's one thing I want you to take away from this book, it's this: Just paying attention to what we are feeling, thinking, and experiencing fundamentally changes it.

The minute we start paying attention to our habits of mind, we react differently to them. Think of it as putting what you do under a microscope. In order to observe something with a microscope, you have to flip on that light under the slide. Just like any other living organism, we react to the light being turned on. It gives us a chance to say *"whoa, there's me back on my bullshit,"* but nicely. Once we start flipping on the light and going *"ah, that's trauma shit"* or *"hey, that's social influence fuckery,"* it makes the rest of the work far easier.

Half of the battle is turning on the light, which is what we've been doing so far in this book, right? Once the psychological shit is put in its proper place, the practical financial work is far more doable. So now we can do the practical work on managing our finances because the psychological shit is being dealt with.

With this light on, we're going to look at unfucking two major areas of our finances here: the what we bring in part and the what we pay out part. My goal here is to give you perspective, point you in the right direction, and remind you to trust your gut and make choices for you and your life . . . not try to create some comprehensive guide to budgeting, choosing your investments, or changing your career.

There's so much financial advice out there on those topics already. How do you figure out what's good and what's bullshit? The first thing I do when I'm looking at advice or some kind of "program" is to read the reviews. But not just what your Uncle Blueford has to say or what the company website has to say. Someone is trying to get you to invest in Amway? First do a google search on "criticism of Amway," "complaints about Amway," "problems with Amway," etc. That's where the tea is really served.

Take even your vetted financial advice with a grain of salt. The Dave Ramsey debt repayment plan that a lot of people use is solid. But the one consistent criticism of it by other financial wonks in the field is his focus on paying off secured debts like mortgages, which most analysts say isn't necessary. So look at what people are saying about the advice you are hearing and also look at how that affects *you*.

Also think about the kinds of emotions the advice is invoking in you. I ask my clients regularly *"Who profits off you feeling this way?"* Do you want to buy this mascara because the advertisement has convinced you that you are ugly? The same goes with financial strategies and investments. If they are being sold to you in some way that in essence tells you that you are a piece of shit but they can fix this for you if you just do as they say? Run like the wind, that's more capitalist hellscape bullshit that we don't have time for.

There is a lot of hard work in this section of the book. But hard work that *you can do*. Work that takes into account your past experiences, the reality of current society, and our goals for unfuckening. And doing this work doesn't mean being hard on yourself for whatever survival techniques you were using up until this point. Whether you have struggled to make a workable budget, to pay down debt, to manage your financial fears, maybe even look at savings and investing strategies, I want you to have tools that make sense. Let's get to work.

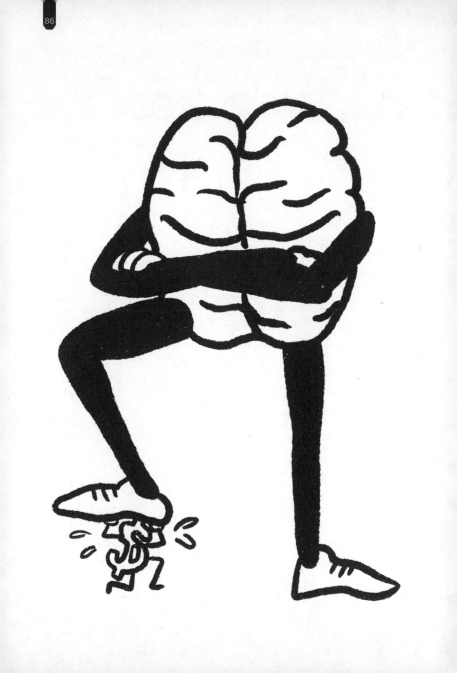

Unfuck Your Spending

S pending money is as much a source of fuckery as earning it. Maybe we overspend for any of the assorted various reasons discussed in the first half of the book. Or maybe we underspend like a dragon sitting on a hoard of gold while only ever eating beans and rice for dinner for the same associated reasons. (What do dragons eat though? Mediocre mid-level execs? Beans and rice are probably healthier if that's the case). Either way, our financial histories can inform unhealthy spending behaviors. And I'm going to address both of these things.

I'm going to start this part of the book with two powerful tools for thinking about your spending, and money in general: Opportunity cost and psychic income.

Opportunity cost

A lot of our focus when we talk about spending is going to be about budgets. They can be hella helpful when planning for a clump of incoming expenses (for a birthday, a holiday, back to school shopping, whatevs). But when we are weighing singular purchases (especially bigger ones that have a decent sized budget impact), there is a great brain hack that has been shown to minimize financial dumbitude and works well with existing budgets.

Because everything has to have a convoluted and non-intuitive name, the hack is called *opportunity cost*.

Opportunity cost refers to the idea that whatever you are spending your money (meaning, your financial energy) on means you are *not* spending it on something else. *Opportunity cost neglect* is what happens when we don't consider the other equally significant possibilities for our use of that financial energy.

For example, let's say it's time to move. Do you decide to spend more on your mortgage and rent so you can have more space or a cooler neighborhood vibe? Maybe the difference is "only" a couple hundred dollars a month . . . and you can afford that. But what else would that $2400 dollars a year buy? Would it pay down the debt you are chipping away at? Allow you to take the vacation you are dying to take? Pay for that class you have had on your mental wishlist for a few years now? Which option provides the best value, in reality? And what about those financial brain traps like mental accounting and social influence from earlier in the book—are any of them coming into play here?

Research demonstrates that being mindful of the opportunity cost of our purchases leads to us purchasing less stuff in general, and not spending nearly as much on the stuff we do choose to purchase. To paraphrase Henry David Thoreau, *the price of anything is the amount of life you exchange for it.*

So basically this means thinking about *all* your spending as an investment, rather than just money flying out into the ether. When you're planning a purchase, your choices really fall into place when you think about whether or not you want to invest your money, the time it took you to earn it, and what else you could use that money, time, and energy for instead.

For you underspenders out there, this concept can help you, too. Financial trauma doesn't just contribute to reactive over-spending. It can also serve as that nasty little voice that devalues our self-worth to the point that we don't ever purchase anything that brings us joy. Or that financial trauma reaction that makes us hoard our gold like a goblin.

And that can turn into a fear of spending anything, which can be just as harmful as overspending. When you're struggling with buying something you need or want, it can also help to consider your money as investing in goals, rather than as buying things you may or may not deserve. Spending a little more money on healthier food leads to a goal of better health (and, honestly, is cheaper in the long run because a crap diet is something our body is going to let us get away with for only so long). And of course doing work on self-compassion is going to go a long way into helping untangle the shitty messages you may have internalized over the years.

Managing the Impulsive Buying Habit

What are your spending triggers? Do you shop when you feel like crap? When you're scrolling social media? When you've had a glass of wine? When you are out with friends and they encourage you to buy the thing you are hesitant about? If you have credit cards in hand? (Yes, research does demonstrate that we will literally spend *double* what we intended to spend if we are using plastic instead of paper, and that's before the interest charges rack up.)

Adulting doesn't mean we have zero bad habits. Adulting means we are able to reverse-engineer our bad habits and do things to keep us from falling into the same traps over and over. Be your own responsibility wing-man and put safeties in place to help you not slide into spending habits that don't align with your other goals and values.

When the impulse-buy gremlins sneak past your wingman of responsibility, check in with yourself:

- Are you in line with the budget you set up for yourself?

- Will buying this thing fuck everything the fuck up?

- Do I need this?

- If it's a want, will it bring a measure of joy to my life?

- Is it something I can *easily* afford?

- I am feeling impulsive or crappy or off kilter and looking for ways to feel better?

- Is there anything else I need to think through?

- If I think better of it later, can I easily return it or am I fucked?

I know it would be super-cool if going down this checklist makes you avoid doing everything dumb for the rest of your life. Unfortunately, there are a lot of forces at work determined to make us buy dumb shit, and nobody is perfect at this. Some people will still go forward and buy that 100th grey sweater (and by some people, I mean me). So when that happens, we gotta face our sweater-buying bullshit and figure out what new protective mechanisms we need to put in place to help support better decision making in the future. There is a reason why some people freeze their credit cards in ice . . . not to self-flagellate, but to slow down their processes long enough to get back in their rational brain. It's okay to get creative when we are fighting for our longer term goals in the face of our short term discomfort and desires.

Psychic income

Another brain hack I want y'all to keep in mind is a concept that economists (with their dumb ass words) call *psychic income*. This brings us back to that early-on statement that money isn't a physical entity in the way our brains typically perceive it. It's a form of energy.

Psychic income is a broad, nebulous category of non-tangible payoffs we get from some kind of economic activity (including our jobs). But because it's important for economics terms to be confusing, psychic income isn't just about what we earn. It's about how we enjoy things in relation to any economic exchange, whether making or spending. So it also refers to the idea that going out for coffee is worth more to you than the coffee you make at home (because, yes, no one is unaware that we could make our coffee at home for less money).

Psychic income is the not-easily-measured form of energy we get from the work we do and the things we use our money on. It could mean spending money on an amazing outfit that fits perfectly and helps you feel powerful. That confidence can go on to influence other areas of your life, making your relationships better. That wasn't something you "bought" when you bought the clothes, it's the psychic income that comes from feeling that you are projecting your best self.

Psychic income is how much more my husband and I enjoy going to a concert or show downtown if we take a ride-share so we don't have to deal with traffic, parking, creepy stairwells in downtown garages in the middle of the night wearing heels (that part's all mine, he doesn't generally wear heels), being stuck trying to get out of the damn parking garage with everyone else, missing the encore to beat the mass exodus, or being stressed about the car getting sideswiped. That is worth way more than the twenty bucks we spend on the Lyft.

Further, the concept of psychic income might include turning down the job that pays $5k a year more because you prefer to work for a non-profit with a mission you believe in. Or maybe the lower-paying job means you don't have to drive on the 405 into work, which saves you a ton in stress and gives you more time to be home with your awesome pet turtle, watching Netflix.

Psychic income is a powerful tool and shouldn't be discounted when looking at how you're spending and making money.

Budgeting as Radical Self-Care

I f you Google "budgeting as self-care" all the results are around how much of your budget should be spent on self care (The Google (™) suggests no more than 5% if you are curious). And how you can do self-care on the cheap if you are totally broke.

I mean, cool.

There's nothing wrong with recipes for at-home pedis or whatever, but what about centering a budget *as* a form of self-care instead of putting self-care *in* a budget? Those search results just solidified something I've noticed about the term self-care in recent years that pisses me off.

Self-care has come to refer only to the fluff. Like bubble baths and sheet masks. And these things are totally fine. And fun. But self-care isn't just fun. Self-care is *the difficult work of centering our own needs so we can maintain our health and well-being.* That's my personal definition (go ahead and steal it if it resonates), but the meta-message is the same as all the dictionary definitions.

Self-care care is the tough stuff. Dealing with our trauma histories. Getting our teeth cleaned. Spending all day on the phone setting up a student loan payment plan. Dealing with the capitalist hellscape with eyes wide open and full awareness. And budgeting. Which is where we're going to start.

Budgeting can be one of the scariest things we do financially. Why? Oftentimes not knowing the full extent of something feels safer. The scientific term for that is *experiential avoidance*. If we perceive something as a threat, we will try to inhibit our emotions and suppress our thoughts around that experience. It's good old-fashioned post-trauma brain wiring again.

So we are going to sneak around our experiential avoidance by starting with the positives. Our values.

Define Your Own (Money) Values

All of the decisions you make about money should be grounded within your value system, not the value system others have foisted upon you. Figuring out what is what helps you determine if you are operating in a healthy money space and if you have enough money to live your values.

So let's start with the following list of things that may or may not have value to you, that are cost-associated (that is, shit we generally have to spend money on to access):

- Transportation (car and related car expenses, bike and biking gear, cab or rideshare fares, bus passes)

- Housing (new place, dream home, vacation home, etc.)

- Renovations/Upgrades/Household Projects

- Art or artisan Supplies made by others

- Books

- Music

- Computer (or other tech) hardware or software

- Games, gaming equipment, tournament entry

- Creative endeavours (art supplies, instruments, recording equipment, etc. either as a business or for the sake of creation)

- Business investments

- Joining and otherwise supporting an organization

- Emergency funds

- Retirement savings/Long term investments

- Sports/Hobbies/Athletics

- Eating out/Social activities

- Paying someone to manage tasks for you (domestic labor, personal assistant, etc.)

- Clothing/Accessories

- Grooming/Personal appearance (regular haircuts, manicures, makeup, etc.)

- Charitable giving (either directly to people in need or through an organization)

- Vacation/Travel

- School/Education/Continued learning (for yourself or a loved one)

- Medical treatments/Surgeries (stuff not covered by insurance)

- Paying down debt

- Paying back someone who helped you in the past

- Spending money generally on others (buying gifts, taking people out to eat, paying for a cousin's econ textbook, etc.)

- Other self-care that isn't covered by insurance (acupuncture, massage, coaching, healthier foods, sexual aids, etc.)

- Tipping well because people are out there working damn hard

Ok, now let's organize them. Add in whatever other categories I left out.

CONSISTENT PRIORITY	SOMETIMES IMPORTANT	EVERY ONCE IN A WHILE	ZERO IMPORTANCE TO ME

Next questions, now that you have your priorities laid out clearly in front of you:

1) If you had an extra $100 dollars, where would it go?

2) What category or categories does that expenditure fall under? (for example, a therapeutic massage might include three categories: "other self care," "tipping well," and "transportation" for a ride-share to and from the appointment.

3) Did the categories align with ones you consider higher priority?

4) If not, was it because of unique circumstances you are currently experiencing?

5) Did you realize that your priorities may be different than what you originally thought?

6) Now what if it's $1000?

7) What about $10,000?

The point of this exercise (and there are more values exercises in the *Unfuck Your Boundaries Workbook* if this kind of thing if your kink) is to blow out the cobwebs of OPP (which, in this case, means Other People's *Priorities*) and re-center in what *your* authentic financial priorities are. If we are going to look at spending habits, reality-based budgets, dream budgets, and the like, they should be centered on what has meaning and joy for *you*.

The next part of budget creation is finding ways to make your, ahem, *values-based* budget happen. When we are looking to do things that are important to our core, authentic selves, that fundamentally shifts how we approach the problem. If our goal is to put money into monthly massages, giving up the monthly sushi in pursuit of our goal doesn't activate our internal obstinance. And having to hunker down on some side-hustles doesn't feel like spitting on a forest fire, because you have a plan in place where you can really see the results of your extra work.

Make a Dream Expenditures List

Now you've done all this work unpacking the stuff that is most important for you to spend money on—good for you. This next exercise isn't about what is possible in the present, but about paying attention to what's important as you move into the future.

List your big ticket wish list items. Things that aren't recurring monthly expenses but require a hefty payout upfront. You define hefty: 100 dollars may be dinner out for some people and an utterly untenable goal for others. Your list might include things like traveling abroad, investing in yoga teacher training, getting your bathtub refinished, fixing your grandpa's antique watch, or whatever else you would like to do if money weren't a consideration.

Now list out the regular monthly expenditures you'd have room for in a dream budget. Things like weekly massages, bi-weekly therapy, a luxe grocery budget that allows for organic purchases, dinners out with friends, or paying down your student loans from hell.

Put a star (or highlight or whatever) your highest priority dream expenditures, both one-time and regular.

Now we have an idea of where we are headed, right? So let's see where we are now in comparison.

Look at Your Current Expenditures

Now make a nice mug of tea, take some deep breaths, and head into this one. No self-shaming, just information, okay? Use your COAL exercise from earlier in the book to help manage any trauma activation, just like you would with any other trauma responses.

Look back over what you've spent in the past 90 days. Detail what money came in and what money went out. Maybe it's because I'm old, but I think this is easiest to do on paper with a color code for expenditures. Come up with a color key so you can see patterns at a glance (like green for bills, pink for food, etc).

Track your spending for a week, as you go along. This is a good tool in becoming more mindful about where your money goes on the regular. What patterns are you noticing? Anything surprised you? Anything out of alignment with your financial values?

I'm including two expense trackers here—the first one is for people with a lot of expenses every day, so you can list them all out with plenty of room. Feel free to make copies (or use a notebook) to record multiple days. The second one fits a whole week onto one page, which may work better for some of you.

After this first week, consider continuing to track your spending. It's helpful to know where your money is really going, and can help hold you accountable to your goals.

Daily Expense Tracker

DATE	EXPENSE	AMOUNT	CASH/CHECK/DEBIT/CREDIT

Weekly Expense Tracker

	EXPENSE	AMOUNT	PAYMENT TYPE
MONDAY			
TUESDAY			
WEDNESDAY			
THURSDAY			
FRIDAY			
SATURDAY			
SUNDAY			

Okay, Let's Make a Starter Budget

You're probably reading this book because you don't currently have a budget in place. If you do, and it's already aligned with your financial values, then you are an utter badass and can skip this part entirely. Go put your feet up and I'll holler when the rest of us are done.

This is just a "where you are right now" budget. It's not your ideal, it's your reality.

You can write your budget right here in this book, copy off the worksheets and shove them in a binder, or grab a separate piece of paper or journal to start planning. Feel free to adjust the categories to work for you and to separate out anything you know is deductible for your small business, or that is related to a value you want to do more or less of.

Total Regular Income

This isn't like the check you got from the car accident insurance settlement, but the regular money you get in that you can rely on month to month.

Paychecks (salary after taxes, insurance, etc is taken out, check cashing fees, etc.). If it varies because of tips or freelance income, look back at your past months and use a lowball estimate or average:

Other regular income (child support, rent from roommates, side hustle income):

Monthly Expenses

Rent/Mortgage:

Renter's or homeowners Insurance (if separate):

Utilities (electricity, gas, water, sewer, trash):

Internet, cable, phones, streaming subscriptions:

Other housing expenses (property taxes, lawn care, housekeeping, HOA fees):

Basic groceries and household supplies:

Special groceries for holidays, celebratory dinners, etc:

Meals out:

Alcohol and other fun substances:

Snacks, treats, and other food/drink expenses:

Books, music, gaming stuff, tech stuff:

Public transportation:

Taxis/Rideshares:

Gas:

Parking/tolls:

Vehicle maintenance (Oil changes, inspections, bicycle repair, etc):

Vehicle insurance:

Vehicle loan:

Other transportation expenses:

Health insurance premiums (if not already accounted for in paycheck):

Payments on balances of past medical expenses:

Medication copays:

Appointment copays:

Other medical care paid out-of-pocket (e.g., acupuncture, neurofeedback, therapy, vision correction, dentist):

Child care/babysitting:

Child support (if not already accounted for in paycheck):

Money given/sent to other family members:

Clothing/shoes/jewelry:

Other personal care expenses (haircuts, pedis, etc):

Laundry:

Activities (movies, museums, glo golf):

Cozy and special occasion household items (candles, Halloween decorations, floofy blankets):

Donations:

Membership expenses (clubs, gym, etc):

Fees for cashier's checks or money orders:

Prepaid cards like phone cards:

Bank or credit card fees:

Other capitalism-based "service" fees:

School costs (school supplies, tuition, student loan payments, gym uniforms, class pictures, that fucking popcorn the PTA sells):

Pet related expenses:

Credit card payments (current minimums):

Investment contributions:

Savings contributions:

Emergency fund contributions:

Other expenditures and fuckery not otherwise specified:

list more:

Unfucking your budget

Ok, this is the extra crying part. The *"if late stage capitalism wasn't a total shit-show I wouldn't have to make ridiculous decisions like this"* part. Let's own that up front. And let me say for the billionth time that it's a shit-show because it's designed to be a shit-show, not because you are a failure.

You're reading this book because you are trying to hold it all together in ridiculous circumstances. We are doing this work to thrive *despite* the system, not because the system is designed for our success.

This "ideal" budget was made popular in the book Elizabeth Warren and her daughter Amelia Warren Tyagi wrote together, entitled *All Your Worth: The Ultimate Lifetime Money Plan.*

Their idea is that 50% of our budget should go toward our needs. Mortgage or rent, utilities, groceries, health care, and minimum payments on unsecured debt (so your credit doesn't end up in the shitter).

The next 20% goes toward building an emergency fund, paying down debt, and other savings or wealth building activities.

Then the last 30% goes to the things that make life worth living. Movies, treats, yummy smelling candles. You know . . . the stuff that you really value and enjoy.

And you may be thinking (or muttering out loud, as I am want to do) *"fuck the fuck off . . . I have a crap ass job in a really expensive city, way more than 50% of my income goes to my needs."* I feel you. And the research backs you up. 50% would be ideal but as Warren and Tyagi wrote in their follow up book *The Two-Income Trap*, the reality is that while in 1973, 50% of discretionary income went to basic living needs, the number today is more like 75% or more.

So if the reality of your current budget is that your basic needs are more like 75%, let's roll with that. Then you can put 10% to savings and debt. And 15% to the stuff you value and enjoy. And if we find wiggle room to move those expenditures close to the 50-20-30 model then that's awesome.

And if your basic needs budget is 100% of your income, or 127% of your income for that matter, I don't for one second doubt it. I have fucking been there. There are tools later in this section in the book designed to help you get out of this cycle and back into a manageable income/expense ratio that is not about just working more hours in a week than actually exist. But for now, knowing this percentage is helpful because it shows you what you have to work with and what needs to give. And that the problem with your budget isn't that you like to drink lattes, because in a just economy, you would be able to afford a fancy coffee *and* have electricity in your house.

Ok. Firstly, let's break down your budget into these three categories. Don't worry about the percentages part right now. Just where everything goes.

Your Budget Breakdown

HAVE TO HAVE IT (NEEDS)	THE FUN STUFF (WANTS)	SAVINGS & DEBT (STUFF)
ITEM:	ITEM:	ITEM:
AMOUNT:	AMOUNT:	AMOUNT:
ITEM:	ITEM:	ITEM:
AMOUNT:	AMOUNT:	AMOUNT:
ITEM:	ITEM:	ITEM:
AMOUNT:	AMOUNT:	AMOUNT:
ITEM:	ITEM:	ITEM:
AMOUNT:	AMOUNT:	AMOUNT:
ITEM:	ITEM:	ITEM:
AMOUNT:	AMOUNT:	AMOUNT:
ITEM:	ITEM:	ITEM:
AMOUNT:	AMOUNT:	AMOUNT:
ITEM:	ITEM:	ITEM:
AMOUNT:	AMOUNT:	AMOUNT:
ITEM:	ITEM:	ITEM:
AMOUNT:	AMOUNT:	AMOUNT:
ITEM:	ITEM:	ITEM:
AMOUNT:	AMOUNT:	AMOUNT:
ITEM:	ITEM:	ITEM:
AMOUNT:	AMOUNT:	AMOUNT:
ITEM:	ITEM:	ITEM:
AMOUNT:	AMOUNT:	AMOUNT:
ITEM:	ITEM:	ITEM:
AMOUNT:	AMOUNT:	AMOUNT:

Ugh. Ok. Now total the three columns up, and figure out what the percentage of your budget it is. You do this by dividing the column total by your total budget. So if the column total is $100 and your total monthly budget is $1000 dollars, 100/1000 equals .1 which is 10%.

Fucking math.

Your Budget Breakdown Totals

	BUDGET TOTAL	% OF TOTAL
HAVE TO HAVE IT (NEEDS)		
THE FUN STUFF (WANTS)		
SAVINGS & DEBT (STUFF)		

So this may have been challenging for ways you expected or in new and surprising ways. That's part of the healing process, paying attention to how this feels. If we ignore it we end up looking for ways to avoid it and then we are back on our bullshit. What did you notice? Anything surprising? What was the most difficult? It's ok to take a break and re-ground yourself before doing the next part.

Prioritizing Within Your Budget

The next step is to prioritize our expenses *within* each of the three categories: Needs, wants, and savings/debt.

We did all that dream budget work for a reason—to center ourselves around what's important to us. Have you been spending money on things that don't actually have value for you? Are there things you want to save up for that are far more important to you than your student loan debt? What do you want to focus on as you start reorganizing your budget?

Maybe you want to start pricing tiny homes, land, and utilities so you can stop paying such high rent and build equity. If so, saving for that and making that happen may make more long-term sense to you than paying off your Visa bill (because the saved rent will knock out that aforementioned visa bill really quickly).

It can be hard to prioritize within each category, so I'll take it step-by-step here.

Prioritizing Within Your Needs

The "Need to Have It" category is the place where we start looking for ways to get ourselves into a 50-20-30 budget breakdown, if possible. This is the stuff that's mandatory—rent, mortgage, utilities, groceries, healthcare, and minimum payments on unsecured debt. I say that knowing it's gross and awful. I'm sorry that you even need to think this way. None of us should have to pay so much attention to an amount of money that is less than what Jeff Bezos earns per *second* (which is $3182 dollars and *seriously* he can go suck a bag of dicks).

We are going to get into more ideas on pwning capitalism and finding ways of accessing things you need (and want) without having to exchange money for them, but for now we're just talking about paying attention to these expenses and how they break down a little bit closer. It may not make a huge, magical difference but every little bit of breathing room helps, right?

We're going to assume that *most* of the "needs" items in your real-life budget are actual needs and that there isn't any wiggle room.

Look at the list of the "needs" in your budget. And look through your bank statement or expense log. Are there any expenditures that you can easily get rid of or extras you can shave down without creating undue hardship in your life, or that you can find a creative way to save on, like sharing wifi with your neighbors or cutting out the wireless hotspot you rarely use? Every little bit helps here. Or maybe there are bigger things you could plan to look into, like moving to a cheaper apartment, or commuting by bike.

Again, I know doing this sucks ass, and not in the fun kind of way. I lived in that space for more decades that I would like to admit. This isn't about choice-shaming, it's about making the best choices for our self-care in the long term with the reality of the ridiculous obstacles fully in mind.

Prioritizing Within Your Debt and Savings

Ready for this? We're going to put that "what you can barely spare" amount—$10 bucks, $100 bucks, whatever—to work on your future. Because no human being should be owned by a credit card or loan company.

Make a Fuck-You Fund

The one thing that all the financial guru peeps agree on, is that the first money you set aside should be an emergency fund. Not paying down your debt, not investing. Just having some fundage for when life hands you a shit sandwich.

The generally agreed upon number is $1000. A thousand bucks will usually cover your auto insurance co-pay if you're in a crash, or the deposit on a new place if your living situation becomes untenable. Or if you need steel-toed boots for work which are $200 bucks and the pair you have got destroyed. Depending on how these types of expenses run in your area, a bit more than a k might make sense. (We're not talking about a really huge crisis which is going to require a lengthy amount of fuckery-management to overcome. For example, a catastrophic medical expense not covered by your insurance isn't going to be something that you are able to knock out with your fuck-you fund.)

Before you do any work toward paying down unsecured debt, build this fund *first*. Otherwise, the next time a crisis hits, it's going back on a high-interest rate credit card or payday loan or some other capitalistic dumpster fire and you are even deeper in the hole we are trying to crawl out of.

So let's say after you did the rest of your budget, after you pay off all your "need" expenses (including the minimums on your credit cards and student loans), you have $100 bucks left for debts and investments. Put that $100 in the emergency fund until you hit the $1000 (or whatever number makes better sense for you). If you have less than $100, put that in, too. Even if it's the 5-spot you found in a pair of jeans you haven't worn in a minute. Try to put something in every month.

If you have to skip a month of saving, don't give up. Pick it up again next month. You're creating something that wasn't there before. And if you suddenly need a root canal and need to spend everything you've saved . . . that's what it was there for (this is one of the hardest things for me to remember, I feel that frustration in my soul). Start again, and give yourself a high five for not needing to put that on a credit card.

A lot of financial people say (and I agree) that you shouldn't abandon the emergency fund once you hit your savings mark. I'd continue socking away money into it, in much smaller amounts, while you pay down debt. Like maybe $10 a month or so. Set a new goal, like having three months of living expenses at your fingertips in case the shit hits the fan, and build towards it slowly.

After you've got your basic fuck-you fund laid down, let's look at what to do with that $100 a month next . . .

Create a Debt Pay-off Plan

Okay, let's list out all your unsecured debt. Here we're looking at credit cards, overdue hospital bills, student loans, etc. We're not looking at your mortgage or car payments.

Now use this list to decide how to prioritize your pay-off plan. There are a couple good options:

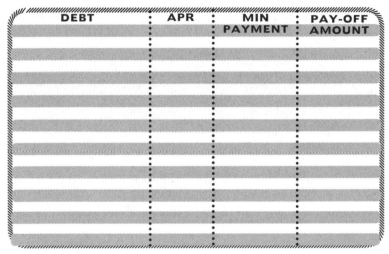

DEBT	APR	MIN PAYMENT	PAY-OFF AMOUNT

SNOWBALL PLAN

This is the plan that was made popular by Dave Ramsey (and most financial advisors agree with his advice, it's generally on point). You start with the debt you owe the least on. Add your savings/debt budget (that hypothetical $100 a month) on top of the minimum payment of that smallest debt and keep paying the minimum on the rest. Once that is knocked out, you put your $100 plus the minimum payment from the first debt, which you are no longer paying, into the next smallest one and so on, with the amount you're able to put towards your debts growing every time.

The snowball plan works because it soothes the tendency for brains to get obsessed with pressing tasks (this is called the Zeigarnik effect if you want to put that in your pocket for trivia night). Research shows that having a plan in place that addresses the pressing task rumination cycle overtly soothes our anxiety. The snowball plan helps you see progress more and more quickly which is both soothing and motivating for further change.

DEBT NAME	TOTAL OWED	MIN PAYMENT DUE	DEBT SNOWBALL AMOUNT	MONTHS TIL PAID OFF
			Min Payment + Extra Cash = Monthly Snowball Amount to Pay	

Instructions:

1. List your debts from smallest to largest. Include name and total owed.

2. List your monthly payment due under Minimum Payment Due

3. Decide how much extra you can put towards debt every month.

4. For the first debt, carry the minimum payment due into the Debt Snowball Amount column.

5. Add that to the extra cash you can pay towards debt in the 4th column to get the Monthly Snowball Amount.

6. Now divide the total owed (column 2) by the Monthly Snowball Amount (column 4) to get the "Months Til Paid Off".

7. Once you finish paying off your first debt, repeat steps 4-6 with the second debt, also adding the minimum payment from the first debt into the extra cash section.

AVALANCHE PLAN

In this payment plan, you focus on the debt that is accumulating the most interest first. If you have debt with some redonk-high interest rates this one may make the most financial sense because it will save you more in the long run.

This is less yummy for our brains in the immediate sense, because you don't see the pay-off progress as fast, but if you calculate the interest you are saving, that may help your motivation level if you are good at recognizing bigger savings over a longer period of time.

Which plan makes the most sense for you, snowball or avalanche? Do you have some ugly-cry-worthy interest rates that you want to tackle head-on? Or does your brain dig the satisfaction of knocking stuff out quickly and having fewer line items to juggle? Figure out which will work best and run with it.

DEBT NAME	TOTAL OWED	MIN PAYMENT DUE	DEBT AVALANCHE AMOUNT	INTEREST RATE	MONTHS TIL PAID OFF

Next-Level Savings

After you've paid down your debt and you have 3 months of living expenses in the bank, what do you do? Other than celebrate this awesome feat of course.

This all depends on your values and goals. Maybe you want to save for retirement or invest generally. This feels waaaaay more complicated than it is for almost all of us. We don't need a financial advisor to make sound investments. It's pretty basic stuff—like if you work for a company that matches your 401K then fuck, yeah start there to collect that match. That's money left on the table if you don't.

Beyond that? One of the best guides I've seen on investing advice is totally free to download, just do a google search for the Bob Veres guide *Finances for My Daughter.* He explains IRAs, index funds, ETFs, and all those options that make grown ass folk cower in fear in very easy to understand terms.

This is not a book about investing (I mean, clearly), but if investing is part of your long-term financial unfuckening goals, know that doing so doesn't have to be at odds with your values, if you want to focus on strategies that contribute to environmental sustainability and social justice, there are resources specific to that end.

Another thing to look at is saving up for larger expenses. Regular, bigger expenses like birthdays and holidays. And then your other value-based goals, like a vacation, a class you want to take, investing in your retirement or your kids' college funds, or buying a house. Remember those bigger-ticket items in your dream budget? That's what your next savings goal is for.

In the finance world, a "sinking fund" is a pool of money that is set aside for something outside of the everyday expenditures. "Sinking" sounds weird and rude, but just refers to the fact that borrowing money for a big ticket expense is referred to in the finance world as "floating" (kinda like asking someone to float you a tenner for lunch). Putting money into a sinking fund is the opposite of borrowing now for something and paying later. Make sense? At least kinda?

More often than not our budgets get blown on things we know are coming. And we can soften the blow if we plan ahead. If not formally with a sinking fund, informally by stretching out the purchases over the rest of the year (I was the queen of shopping for my kids off-season and putting it aside for birthdays, holidays, and back to school) based on the budget you put together now.

There's a planning sheet in the workbook to help figure out your sinking fund needs. Or you could just list out all the far-off expenses you can see coming from here. You're on a roll, so keep at it . . . even if you are looking at vacations, or holidays, or events that are months or years away. Badasses plan that far in advance, and you are clearly a badass. Then divide the total you expect to spend by the number of months you have, and either set that money aside or start making the purchases

Getting Professional Financial Help

What if you are overwhelmed by all this getting-out-of-debt stuff and you need help? That's what credit counselors are for. The National Foundation for Credit Counseling (NFCC.org, y'all . . . there ya go) is a not-for-profit that has credit counselors in every state in the US that can help you go through all your finances and create a plan for fixing them. I did this with my late husband about twenty years ago, because he brought a lot of financial issues into the marriage from his previous marriage. It was *really* helpful and not nearly as awful and shaming as I thought it would be.

A credit counselor's sole job is to get you out of debt. A financial advisor, however, is there to help you build up your net worth.

It used to be that financial advisors were just for people who had huge investment portfolios. There are a lot more options out there now for us normal people, and many financial advisors will work with you as a consultant to help you get on the right track (especially helpful when you have a partner and this is a problem you are tackling together). The idea is to figure out what goal you want to achieve and then find a financial planner who can help you do that.

How much does this all cost? The old rule of thumb was a financial advisor generally charged a yearly fee that was 1% of the assets of your portfolio. So if you had a million dollar portfolio (hahaha, I know), the financial advisor would make 10K a year to manage it. Nowadays, if you want to have a full financial plan put together with a financial advisor, you are looking to spend $500 to $2500 dollars, and they only charge a percentage of the portfolio if they are going to be managing it for you. If you want a consultation on a specific issue, you are looking at a fee of $100-$400 bucks.

Where do you find this person? There are financial planning networks online that will let you search for people in your area who are vetted to provide the service you are looking for.

The biggest thing to consider is that you want a financial planner who is a *fiduciary*. Oy, the things you are learning today, right? Fiduciary is a word that means *trustee*. Essentially, a fiduciary is someone that holds a legal and ethical obligation to be trustworthy to do what is in your best interest over their own. It's considered the highest standard of care in the business world, because they will make financial recommendations based on your needs instead of theirs.

If you are thinking *"Wait, what? Isn't that the job of ALL financial advisors?"* the answer is no. There are advisors that make their money on commission . . . that is getting you to invest in certain plans that make them the most dollars. It's not a shitty or sketch thing (a lot of people live their lives off commission sales) . . . but if what you really need right now is to get a better financial game plan going, buying into a specific deal is definitely not your priority at the moment.

Prioritizing Within the Fun Stuff

This should be the easy part, right? But I've seen people (and by *people*, I mean *me*) have the hardest time with this category. Since it's fun, it becomes mindless. While yes, I do entirely agree in the Church of Everlasting Life and Treating Oneself, I do also believe that these treats need to stick within a certain portion of our budget (you know, the 30% thing again).

This is the time to think about what you truly enjoy the most and prioritize that. If you love having a nice barista make your coffee for you in the morning, that's totally cool . . . make that a priority. If you are lusting after a new smart watch, though, making your espresso stovetop can allow you to sock away the fun money to get one.

Do you want to travel more? Do you like being able to splurge on new shoes? Do you do better if you go to a gym to workout versus work out at home? Do you like seeing movies in the theatre or are you fine with whatever is on Netflix? Thinking about the stuff that makes you happy and weighing them against each other, just like any other aspect of your budget, will help you not overspend *and* lessen your FOMO.

Treating Oneself Well and Often, but, Alas, with Well Defined Limits
First of all, go back to your dream budget list and copy off all the "fun stuff" items you had added.

Ok, cool. So now I want you to rank everything on that list as a 1, 2, or 3. 1 being highest priority, 2 is a mid-range fun having thing, and 3 as a lowest priority. Got it? Now, list the first three "1" items below along with its estimated monthly cost:

Fun Thing:

Super Fun Thing:

Also Deeply Cool:

Now where is your budget at? Room to add some more "1"s? Go ahead and budget them out below:

Got a plan? Badass. The important thing here is that this is a living document, just like every other aspect of your budget. The goal is to be more mindful of your choices everywhere in your budget. And the fun part of the budget tends to be the first place mindfulness goes out the window. You may realize your priorities are shifting and changing and you want to move stuff around. Or your fun stuff tends to be bigger-ticket, so you want to lower your monthly fun allowance and save up for it.

Save Money By Doing Instead of Not Doing
One of the fundamental truths about human nature is that it is always easier to start doing something than to stop doing something. Eating poorly? Add the good foods and let the less-healthy stuff find its own way out of your diet. Overly critical? Focus on saying positive things and watch the criticisms wander off on their own.

Same is true with saving money. If you are looking to cut expenses in one of your categories, add new purchases and activities that are free or cheaper to your day and let them naturally replace the stuff you spend money on now. This feels more like a fun challenge rather than deprivation and limitation.

This could also work for your Needs budget, but starting with Fun Stuff is lower stakes.

Find three cost saving fun activities that you can engage in as an add-on rather than a replacement. Try this for a week and check in. Did the budget expenditure you were hoping to reduce show a decrease this week? Might it over time? Was it easier to make the switch using this method? Do you think you can carry forth this method in other ways?

Unfucking capitalism

So we discussed all the things we typically access through an exchange of money. When we want better groceries, we go to the bougie grocery store and shell out extra money for them.

But part of budgeting should really be finding ways to get our budgetary needs met outside of the capitalistic hellscape. You know, in the ways that all humans managed their needs in the past, and how many people still manage their needs.

I'm talking about exchanging other forms of energy and resources so we can stretch those budgets without going without. This feeds back into that dream budget list. There may be a lot of things that feel out of reach without a fuck-ton more money but that isn't necessarily the case.

This can be rough. You're already busy. You're already fucking exhausted. You are already spending way too many hours working to just barely scrape by and here I am suggesting you add more work to your life through some kind of co-op situation.

Sorta. Also sorta not.

The idea behind an energy exchange is that we are paying for everything out of hours of our life, in one way or another. And when we are working for money and then using that money to purchase what we need and want we are generally operating in isolation from others while a direct energy exchange gives us the opportunity to make social connections and see an immediate benefit of our labor.

Researchers are getting hip to this notion and have started studying it directly. For example, gardening is way more time consuming than buying food at the store (and surprisingly not terribly money saving for most of us . . . says the woman who grows tomatoes solely for the squirrels who live in the tree out back, apparently). But a meta analysis (which means a study combining all the other studies available) on the benefits of gardening found enough that we should be grubbing it up in the dirt, including reductions in depression and anxiety and increases in life satisfaction, quality of life, and sense of community.

There are a zillion ways of meeting your wants and needs without an exchange of money and plenty of books devoted specifically to this topic, but it bears looking at while you are in the budget-adulting zone.

Never stop thinking creatively about opportunities to lower your expenses (and, you know, increase that psychic income). It's far easier to access options in larger cities than small towns, so your options may be limited, but some searching and asking around may collect you up some resources that you hadn't thought of.

Saving on Services

Healthcare. Do you have any low cost care clinics? Have you been putting off expensive dental work that you might get done cheaper at the local dental school? Can you access your local Lion's Club to get glasses? Have you checked NeedyMeds.org to see if there is a prescription assistance plan for your ridiculously expensive meds— or GoodRx for coupons? Have you checked on payment plans for shit you are needing or wanting to get done? Even like a pre-payment plan, like dental layaway or whatever?

Professional services. What kind of pro-bono legal services are available? Are there legal aid organizations in your area? Is it possible to negotiate on the fees for professional services? I've had a lot of success in getting a discount if I'm paying something down immediately. Are their other financial assistance programs? Can you do volunteer work in exchange for a discount? A friend of mine got almost the entirety of her yoga therapy training covered by doing volunteer work for the organization that provides the training . . . score. This isn't true just of not-for-profits, plenty of businesses offer similar deals. It doesn't hurt to ask your local gym if you can help out with a big event they are throwing in exchange for some free membership credits, for example.

Contract work. While the primary purpose of the NextDoor app is to find out which of your neighbors are racist, its secondary purpose is to find people who can get shit done for far cheaper than hiring a company. (That sounds like I'm ordering a hit on someone, though I just meant I paid my neighbor to install my new toilets rather than pay Lowes to subcontract the job out and take most of the money I paid them off the top).

There are a billion other ways of creating barter arrangements in formal and informal ways. Timebank.org allows you to provide services for credits. If you want to organize a barter group in a formal way, the website Grassrootsgrantmakers.org has a really good starter guide. But I have participated in all kinds of more informal bartering relationships my entire life, allowing me (and everyone involved) to access resources that were important to them without having it to impact their $$$$ budget.

It's possible to trade for a lot of services: babysitting, lawn care, etc. My long time friend/hair queen has been looking to offer more holistic care options in his west side neighborhood and suggested I teach yoga in exchange for the haircuts I usually just pay him for. Everybody wins.

Saving on Food, Clothes, and Other Basics
One of the big things I see people say all the time is that they want to eat healthier, and healthy foods are ridiculously expensive (because broccoli isn't a subsidized commodity). More and more people are looking to find ways to feed themselves and their loved ones without having to hand over the entirety of their paycheck to a Jeff Bezos-owned Whole Foods. You may not have space for a garden, but you might have the option of joining a community garden. Or have some windowsill herbs and tomatoes going. Hell, you can even grow sprouts and microgreens indoors as long as you don't have asshole cats as roommates.

There is pretty much a mechanism to rent or borrow anything nowdays . . . even designer clothes, because formal events are just dumb expensive.

Produce bartering. I belong to a neighborhood crop swap where I swap herbs and herbal remedies for veggies and eggs from local people. It's also been a cool way of connecting with people I wouldn't have met otherwise. Fun fact: The guy who supplies me with eggs has a daughter who works in my same field, and I was able to help her find a job when she was new to town and didn't have any connections.

Free food programs. Besides the obvious food banks, there are also programs like Food Not Bombs (generally in larger cities) that also help people access healthy food even when they don't have the financial means. There are more and more food delivery programs that are working to make healthy food accessible. These programs can vary widely depending on where you live so searching online and asking other people what services they use and what they think of them is a good start.

Cooking clubs. For some people, the eating-healthy part isn't even so much the ingredient purchasing, but the time to cook or the know-how around making healthy things. Maybe partner up with someone who does the cooking if you provide the ingredients (or vice versa) . . . or plan cooking/baking/preserving/freezing dates with a buddy to prepare some healthy meals to eat throughout the upcoming month. Check out MeetUp and social media for possibilities (or maybe post a message that you are looking to start one!)

Freecycle and Buy Nothing Groups are neighborhood based groups on social media where people post what they have available and you make plans to collect it and offer up your unwanted or surplus belongings to the group in exchange. These tend to be established in most places, at least in bigger cities. You can usually find them through a Google search or on Facebook.

Community/curbside free boxes. This is de rigour in PDX (so cool) and more common than you'd guess in San Antonio where I live (maybe especially in my neighborhood?) but less common in other parts of the world. But rather than trashing things, or donating them to a corporate thrift chain . . . why not put things out for your neighbors to snap up? I've gotten so much cool shit by "shopping" curbside, and put out goodies for rehoming on the regular. I only live a couple of hours from the border, and have many neighbors with relatives south of it. One guy collects things to take to his family members in Mexico to help out. I'm all for that.

Clothing swaps. This is a party where everyone pools their unwanted or wrong-size but still wearable clothes, tries things on, and takes home whatever they like. You can also informally pass around used clothes, books, and other possessions among friends.

Libraries. Buddha bless libraries. And double plus bless them for offering far more than books to borrow. Many offer movies, music, classes, tickets to local museums and zoos, and so many other things. I read an article about a library that lets people check out specialty cake pans and other kitchenware and that totally made my heart sing.

And I don't just mean your regular municipal library. There are plenty of alternative libraries. Where I live, the worker's union maintains a library (that I donate my books and zines to) and the city maintains a garden "tool library" for people to check out lawn mowers and weed eaters and the like for their weekend garden projects.

We need more village-building in this regard. If you need a book for class (and you know you won't ever use that shit again), ask on Facebook if anyone has it and is willing to let you use it for a few weeks. Trying to cook more at home but have a ridiculous work schedule? Check with your friends to see if anyone has one of those cool crock-pots with the "keep warm" function before you shell out for one at Target.

Put your requests out there to your friends and on social media, the worst you will get is crickets. But you may get some cool shit to try out.

How to Personally Unfuck Capitalism

- What talents/resources do you have that you can share?

- What talents and resources do others have that would save you fundage if you could access them?

- What are some ways of spreading the word? (e.g., posting on facebook that you will help people do their taxes in exchange for a vitamix blender that's gathering dust in their pantry)

Money, Relationships, and Boundaries

So far in this part of the book we've talked about budgeting and spending money as though you're making all these decisions totally solo. But we have to negotiate money with other people all the time. Everything from how much allowance the kids get (and what they're allowed to spend it on) to who's paying for college or the nursing home. Between roommates over the rent and utilities and any other shared bills. Between friends negotiating a bar tab or if one person always wants to do stuff the other person can't really afford. The coworker who always wants a ride but never chips in for gas. Money is already awkward to figure out internally, and now you need to negotiate with a whole other human being and *their* money bullshit. Fuck.

Communicating effectively about money and your boundaries around money is tough. In the U.S. we talk about money about as effectively as we talk about sex. That is, it's all innuendo and braggadocio, and very little pragmatic, thoughtful dialogue.

I mean, no wonder it's a hellscape, right? So how do we change that? Face-fucking-forward because we are tired of this dumb bullshit, right?

Money and Partnership

Ok, so you have a partner. No matter what the dynamic is (committed, casual, or . . . um . . . complicated), statistically speaking money is causing some kind of conflict. Money is the number one thing that couples argue about and the number two cause of divorce (the number one cause is actually infidelity but I'm going to say it's not letting your wife rescue any more cats because apparently four cats is plenty).

The most important two things about resolving your financial issues in your relationship are communication—having upfront conversations about how money is being allocated—and a commitment to *financial fidelity*. This is just like sexual fidelity—it means whatever rules you agree on for the relationship, you both honor them. A budget made with a partner is a contract. Nobody is perfect, but continuous fuck-ups are a pretty big hit on a relationship.

I work with a lot of couples going through separation and divorce, and sketch shit about money is a problem that comes up over and over again as relationship enders. Small things like constantly going out to lunch with work buddies when there was a commitment to bring sacked lunches in order to pay down debts, or trips to Target where the packages stay hidden in the trunk of the car. Or big ones, like money being hidden and accounts being emptied.

If you're having money conflict in your relationship, the first step is to figure out what kind of help you need. Are your relationship's financial problems communication shit or chronic financial infidelity shit? Even if you're not sure, I'd high-key recommend starting with therapy (couples counseling if you can convince your partner to go). All the practical financial advice on the planet won't help if one member of the agreement continues to say one thing and do another. And financial conflict is definitely a type of relational conflict, so if you have health insurance that covers therapy, it'll be covered. If you are looking for free or low-cost options in your community, lead in with the fact that it is a relational conflict, rather than saying you are looking for financial counseling.

Even if you aren't hiding things from each other, how do you negotiate money in your partnership when, say, one of you is an overspender and one is an underspender? Or if you have different values around tipping, or different priorities in paying down debt or what to save for, or whether to save at all?

First you gotta create a budget y'all can live with. Like separately, without breathing down each other's neck, use the tools from earlier to figure out your priorities while your partner does the same. Then sit down and share your results.

Start with where you agree and plan around that. Even if the only thing you agree on is that paying your rent is better than being evicted.

Then negotiate on the stuff where you disagree. You know, the fun stuff like buying a new house versus using the extra for trips. I know, this can be rough. It can be helpful to discuss your short and long term goals as individuals and as a team. When money is the relational point of contention for couples and families in therapy, these are the conversations that I start with.

After that heavy lifting has been done one of the big things that really helps is making sure that everyone in the relationship has a guilt-free discretionary fund, where what you spend it on isn't challenged. Even if it's ten dollars that you want to be able to use on onion rings or puffy stickers, having some financial fun is important. It could be money that's put aside into a separate account or cashed out for walking-around, but it needs to be all yours. Feeling like you're under your partner's microscope is no fun for anyone. It's a partnership, not a parent-child relationship, after all. I mean, unless that's your kink, which is totally cool by me.

It's also helpful to set a dollar amount on other household expenses, where purchases over that amount are discussed. This may be for small things, like the grocery budget, and larger things like buying a new bike or car. Giving your partner the chance to weigh in on *"I found this thing for $200 more than we planned on spending but I think it makes sense because . . . ..what do you think?"* will save infinite fights later, trust Auntie Faith.

If your communication is good and y'all are in a good *same team* mindset to make some financial changes together, you can still get financial assistance and it doesn't have to cost a dumb amount of money. All the information earlier about credit counseling and financial advisors totally applies to teamwork finances, not just individual finances.

Other People Fucking Up My Finances

Partners aside, how your friends and family spend their money—and expect you to spend yours—can definitely impact you and cause you stress. Buddies go out drankin' all the time? Family that buys expensive ass gifts and you are expected to reciprocate? We have all had an experience of getting pulled along with some spending that we hadn't budgeted for, really couldn't afford, and resent later.

It's most helpful to realize in advance which of these situations are the ones that are you most likely to get stuck in so you can organize your counter-attack in advance. If you have a plan in place and a script to rely on, you are far less likely to end up pulling out your wallet and fucking up your whole financial month.

Some ideas to get you started:

- "I'm doing an austerity month challenge so I have to pass on the concert this month. But I've been all up into my free-event research and the museum is free next Sunday, wanna plan a paintings and picnic date with me?"

- "We've been looking at our long term financial goals and made some changes so we can achieve them at a faster rate, so we've decided to opt out of the family gift exchange this year. Honestly, our favorite part is just hanging out with everyone, please don't feel the need to buy us any gifts . . . Auntie Enid's chess pie is what we live for, and we promise to bring the lemon bars!"

- "That sounds like a blast, but I'm determined not to bust out my plastic this month . . . can I skip the dinner and join y'all for the movie part after? That'll save me a ton of fundage and honestly, I want to finish off these leftovers before they spoil so I can be proud of frugal adulting prowess."

- "I get mad at myself every year that I can't go on vacation, and I'm determined to make it happen this year . . . so I'm gonna pass on the outlet mall trip. I know me, and I don't make good choices once I have the opportunity to buy my 100th grey sweater."

These are all matter-of-fact examples that focus on your financial goals with zero shame attached to other people's choices. And that's the way it should be, right? If people wanna drop some bills on tequila shots, that's 100% their right. But being thoughtful and practical about *your* choices may end up starting a trend with some of your people. Your friends may say "Oh! What's an austerity month? (There's more on that in the workbook if you're interested.) Maybe we could all do that together and support each other!" Maybe your family will say "Good idea! Let's do a cookie swap or a white elephant exchange rather than spend fifty bucks on brandy snifters!" Or whatever. Brandy snifters are a thing right? I dunno. The point is, you aren't asking anyone to do anything different because of your spending changes.

I say several times a week in my office that it isn't that people aren't willing to *change*. We are just unwilling to *be changed*. Frame it as *your* thing, rather than something everyone should do with you. Because even if that is 100% not your intent, people will read it as such unless you state quite clearly that you don't give AF how they spend *their* money. If you make all these changes and they're still sitting around with their brandy snifters, whatever. You aren't pushing your choices onto others, and are working to find ways to stay connected without dropping a ton of dough. Be like the vegan who brings an amazing plant-based chili to a pot-luck and offering no side-eye to all the meat based dishes other people bring.

But Faith, you're thinking. What if they are shitty about it? Or passive aggressive? Yeah. People do that shit. And it's about them, not you. And if it's their shit, you don't have to take it on. It's totally cool to recognize and validate that they don't like what you're doing and do it anyway. *"Be that as it may, I'm sticking to my plan for now. If it doesn't work out you can laugh at me later!"* is a cheerful, argument-ending answer.

The other big issue we tend to get into with our friends and family members is when they want to borrow money. This is tough. You've done a lot of work on getting your own shit together and then you have people around you saying "cool, hook me up." I was raised in a culture where caring for your community is a core value. So I believe in that. And I get it. But caring for your parents or siblings shouldn't come before caring for yourself and/or planning for your own kiddos.

I'm a big believer in not lending money I can't afford to lose. I would rather give someone the money they need outright and not set up a resentment trap for the both of us. I know that for some people, paying back a loan is really important to them (that's me, I'm some people), so I won't insist on making it a gift, but I still operate as if the money is gone and spent and not going to be returned.

I also don't want to get hitched into an ongoing problem. A family member recently asked my husband to co-sign for a line of credit so they could deal with a credit card collections demand. After my husband and I discussed it, we offered the money to get them caught up on the current credit card instead of having our name on a janky payday type loan.

If you love someone but don't really trust them to spend money on what they say it's for, then is it possible to just buy them the thing they say it's for? If a family member can't make rent . . . can you write the check to their landlord rather than fork over the cash? It's your money, you get to make the rules and set the boundaries.

When someone tries to hit you up, it's okay to take a minute to respond. Tell them "let me look and see what's possible" or "let me talk to Boo about what bills we have coming up and get back to you." That gives you some breathing space so you don't feel pressured into making an immediate decision. *Then* decide what you can and are willing to do and make that offer.

And then? Tough as it is? Remember what I said in *Unfuck Your Boundaries*: "No" is a complete sentence.

Unfuck Your Income

I f we are talking about money and how it affects our daily lives, we'd be remiss if we didn't talk about how we actually get the money into our pockets.

So *what* we have and earn and *how* we have and earn it is a really important part of the discussion. Especially for those who have so much of our life's meaning and purpose tied into their jobs or careers (and I'm not dissing that at all, I'm one of them).

We are going to talk mostly about *work* in this chapter, because that's where most of us get our income and is the source of income we have some modicum of control over.

There are many other ways of accessing income. It can come from child support or alimony, various government programs, our families (whether that's a trust fund, a one-time inheritance, or the relative with the fancy job who helps out when there's a rent shortfall), investments, insurance settlements, tax refunds, mutual aid and disaster relief, crowdfunding for medical expenses., etc.

I'm not dismissing any of these methods. I think it's important to recognize that there can be stigma and shame attached to them, which has no place in a cultural revolution. There shouldn't be shame in accessing the help you need when you need it. I mean, if billion dollar companies are getting bailed out with our tax dollars, there is nothing wrong with feeding our fucking kids with food stamps.

Says the woman who fed her fucking kids with food stamps.

Ahem. But anyway, small rant aside, this part of the book is going to be focused on how to unfuck exchanging your labor for money. That might mean making a bad job bearable, finding a new job, or starting something for yourself.

Get a new job

While this isn't a book about finding your passion and embarking on a new career trajectory, we do gotta talk about it at least a little bit, right? Our biggest connection to income for most people is our careers. And our self worth absolutely becomes impacted in both positive and negative ways in the process. I'm all about the practical, so I want to spend a little time discussing the job hunting skills that everyone should have been taught in high school, but didn't. Let's get real for a few pages.

Knowing Your Worth

How much income *should* you be earning? How much is your time and energy and labor worth?

I mean, the capitalistic hellscape runs on maximizing profit. And maximizing profit means minimizing expenses. Including human labor. Rare is the place that is going to appropriately compensate you without a damn battle.

Then there is those of us who work in not-for-profits, community agencies, and the like and we are often there because we value being of service more than making fuck-tons of money . . . .and while a lot of these agencies are legitamately running on a shoe-string, many more are taking advantage of their workers, knowing that they are huge-hearted humans who are passionate about the work they are doing.

So before we get into some practical advice, I want you to push out that modesty zone and *go to town* on why you are an utter badass at the work you do.

What Do You Bring to the Table?

Grab that special notebook and write down all the cool things you can do and how they provide value for the company you work for.

- Education and Training?

- Experience?

- Hustle?

- Personality traits and other cool shit that enhance your workplace value (creative problem solver, likeable, schedule flexibility, etc.)?

- Regular job duties . . . like every-damn-thing at work you are responsible for?

- The extra stuff you do that you aren't even responsible for but you do anyway because you're a badass like that?

Ok, good. Now that you have *in writing* what you bring to the table in terms of talent and ambition, we are going to talk about how to translate that into unfucking your income.

Thinking About a New Job (Or a Whole New Career)?

Are you considering getting a new job? Statistically, you probably are. Research done by people at Indeed (you know, the job hunting website), found that 71% of people are either looking for or open to a new job. And it's not just people who are over the bullshit of somewhere they have worked for a really long time. Indeed also found that 65% of people are looking for a new job within three *months* of starting one. And that's generally the higher earners. When they broke it down, 50% of the people making six figures are looking for the next step up the food chain within thirty *days* of starting a new job.

My take on this? If high earners are hustling constantly and looking for the next big thing before they have even found the break room at the place that just hired them, you are not being a ridiculous human for considering the same ... but then why is it so difficult to have the same level of confidence as some mediocre middle management executive?

Considering making a change is the hardest part of the process for people, according to research. The things that jam us up are considered part of *prospect theory*, which is how we analyze decisions that have a measure of risk. According to prospect theory, there are two negative biases that humans have that get in the way of starting the job-search process. The first is that we overestimate our chances of failure and we underestimate the benefits of making a change.

That is why making career decisions is a high-stress life event for human beings. On one life stressor measurement, changing careers is *more* stressful than having your home foreclosed on.

So in all the steps it takes to move from your current job to a new job (whether new career field or not), making the decision to be an active applicant is the hardest one. The best way to overcome that hurdle is to feel in control of the process. This means doing your own research, rather than listening to others. Earlier I encouraged you to embrace your awesomeness and lay out what you bring to the table. Now is your chance to think about where you want to bring it.

Finding Your Meaning
The best way I've found to approach a job or career switch, is to focus on what engagement looks like at a personal level. Which brings us to the work of Christina Maslach. Dr. Maslach is a social psychologist/badass who is known professionally for two big things. The first is that she stopped the Stanford Prison Experiment (see? badass) and the second is that she spent decades researching occupational burnout.

She was originally measuring burnout in people who worked in human services, then realized that it fits *all* jobs. She created an assessment tool called the Maslach Burnout Inventory, which is an extremely long list of all the factors that culminate in burnout, as well as all the factors that define the opposite of burnout: engagement. In developing her theory of *engagement*, which is what keeps us happily engaged in whatever we're doing, she defined it as the sum of three different experiences: *energy*, *involvement*, and *efficacy*. These factors held true throughout the world, it wasn't just a U.S. thing.

Of course I could unpack what energy, involvement, and efficacy looks like (there is a fuck-ton of research on them), but honestly, all of these are very individualized, internalized processes. What is energizing for me would be sensory overload for my partner (the ever-patient Mr. Dr. Faith). If you're thinking about changing your job or career path, it's a good idea to spend some time considering what makes you feel energized, involved, and effective. Let's start with these questions that focus on what work engagement looks like for you.

WORK ENGAGEMENT QUESTIONNAIRE

- Would you work if you didn't have to?

- Would it be the same work that you are doing now? If so, how would it be different?

- What kinds of work situations do you find yourself in that you work harder than you have to?

- What kinds of activities are most likely to make you think *"THIS. This is my contribution to making the world suck less?"*

- Are there any situations where you would work for less than your "normal" pay? What makes those situations different for you?

- What kinds of things do you do when you have no obligations and free time?

- If you were able to schedule your working time anyway you would like in a 7 day week what would your calendar look like?

- What are you "known for" at work, among your family, among your friends? Like, what are the go-to types of problems that people rely on you to solve or assist them with solving?

These questions are important ones to look at *before* planning for a switch. I have seen people jump from one shit job into the dumpster fire of another because they were so desperate to leave one hellscape that they didn't see where they were going. And not only have I seen other people do it, I have done it wayyy too often myself. Different isn't necessarily better. If you are going to invest in new job training and the like, being thoughtful and proactive minimizes the risk of the same bullshittery in a new and different outfit.

The aforementioned Mr. Dr. Faith made a similar leap a little over a year before I wrote this book. He found more and more joy in community organizing and volunteer activities and started exploring a career change. He had been in auto claims for decades (which is the soul-sucking shit-show you would imagine). The opportunity came up for him to train and become certified as a peer recovery coach. This option resonated. He has his own experience with addiction and recovery, and has seen how vital peer recovery specialists are to the health care system. The ultimate outcome? He recently celebrated his first year working for a community mental health organization as a recovery coach and case manager.

What Next? Why Next? When Next?

Spend some time thinking—write it out or make a vision board (check out my *Vision Boarding* zine for some help with that) or whatever.

- What's on the agenda? New job? Same or different org? Whole new career?

- What is the impetus for the change?

- What would it take to do so?

- What is the best-case scenario payoff?

- Still thinking this might be a good plan?

- What's the first step to making a change?

Ok, hotstuff. Now make a commitment to taking that first step. Write that shit down and give yourself a due date. Get an accountability buddy on board. Go all in like mediocre mid-level managers!

Having Your Worth Recognized

Negotiating your wage or salary when you change jobs or asking for a raise at your current job is the number one work-related stressor I hear about from my clients. So I wanted to give some special attention to that topic.

Remember all the work you did, listing out your attributes and bad-assery? Now it's time to ask for appropriate compensation for all of them.

I have zero idea why some companies are not up front about what they are offering for a particular position. It is a total waste of THEIR time, not just the applicants, to weed through all that correspondence, set up interviews, interview candidates, and then be told *"Hahahaha, that's the pay? No."* Unfortunately, that's the norm in most places so you have to be prepared to interview without that info.

What kind of salary range are you supposed to come up with when they ask? Definitely prepare for that question ahead of time. If you have colleagues in the field, ask them what would be reasonable. You can also get good information on salary ranges for positions in the area you live on websites such as GlassDoor.

But honestly? The best trick is to high-ball your range. The Columbia School of Business conducted a study on salary ranges, and found that when people listed the amount they actually wanted as the lowest point on their range, they got offered far better compensation packages.

Try to get as much info as possible in the interview so your time isn't wasted, even if they want to waste theirs. This includes all the aspects of the compensation package that are important to you. Straight up lead with what your priorities are and what other obligations you have. I would use something like:

> *I know the salary range is influenced by many factors, but I was hoping to get a general idea of what it might be. Of equal importance to me are the health care benefits and the schedule stability. I'm a widow with two kiddos so good benefits are really important. As is making sure that I am able to get out of work on time to see their football games, teach at the local university as an adjunct, blahblahblah.*

I had plenty of jobs over the years where the flexibility I needed to care for my family made up for a salary that wasn't ideal. Being able to flex out my schedule, or work from home, or whatever, was vitally important, as was communicating that upfront. This is important whether you're negotiating a salary and benefits or just a straight up hourly wage.

There may be other benefits that are specific to your field. You might ask if you can get assistance with licensing and certification expenses? Let you learn more about your field on their dime or at least on the clock? If you are driving for work, are they providing reimbursement and/or assistance with car maintenance? Have assistance with uniforms, footwear, or other work gear?

In many organizations (especially not-for-profit orgs) there are different piles of money that are earmarked differently. There may not be any wiggle room on your salary, but there could be room to negotiate on benefits, or thousands of dollars available for you to get a fancy certification that you can use to vault into a better paid position down the line.

Unfuck Your Current Job

Maybe your job is okay. You know, it's fine. It is what it is. But it isn't what you want to be doing. Maybe you're barista-ing your way through school. Or temping during the day so you can afford the roof over your head while writing or making art at night. It would be great to make enough from the creative part but you aren't there yet. Or maybe the career path that seemed exciting when you got your current job is slowly sucking your soul away. And it's a bummer.

Or maybe you love your job, maybe it's even exactly what you want to do with your life . . . but the job circumstances suck ass. There are so many ways a job can suck: your boss is terrible, or you are working under unsafe conditions, or the company isn't supportive of your identity, or your coworkers are assholes, or the work you do makes the world a worse place, or, or, or . . . .

So what do we do with all that?

I'm going to draw on some buddhism here to talk about the concept of *livelihood*, which is a fancy way of saying how you make your money. Livelihood, for my non-Buddhisty people, is a core element of the Noble Eightfold Path of the Buddha. The Buddha's answer for what to do with your livelihood was a pretty strict one. He said that practicing Buddhists should not engage in the following types of business: making, selling, or distributing weapons, the trafficking or slavery of other human beings, anything around the business of meat, anything around the business of intoxicants, and anything around the business of poisons. If you look up modern interpretations of right livelihood, they usually include more conceptual values like justice, equality, and environmental sustainability.

How many people can say that they are genuinely in compliance with right livelihood? And for those of us who can, how many of us can say it has been so throughout our lives? I mean, we are calling it a capitalist hellscape for a reason, right?

How many people out there actually get to do a job that they genuinely love, day in and day out? Not many of us. And probably not you if you are experiencing enough frustrations to pick up this book, right?

In *Standing At The Edge* by Roshi Joan Halifax,), she talks about *edge states*. This is a term that Roshi Joan coined to explain the psychological territories that are essential for good humaning, but can easily turn toxic if we aren't aware and proactive about our bullshit.

In that book was a small section, like four paragraphs long, on right livelihood. And she says *what* we do and *why* we do it are only part of our livelihood. And equally (or perhaps even more) important is *how* we do it. No matter what our job, we can approach it with integrity and create meaning within that experience.

And I'm not just saying this from the perspective of the job I have now. My first job out of college was as a Subway sandwich artist. Clearly I wasn't chuffed about this, because I had Big Plans to change the world. So instead I made it my mission to learn as much as I could from the experience. Not just budget management, but how to care for *people*. My crew, my customers. Maybe I wasn't working in my field, but I could still create space for people to be seen, heard, and cared for. Often that just meant remembering them and what was important to them and making human connections.

I'm not saying this to say "be grateful and count your blessings if your job is shit." A shitty job is shitty, full stop. (And that job was legitimately pretty ass in many ways.) I didn't regret leaving that job when I landed a position that allowed me to do the work I was passionate about. But I also learned, first hand, the meaning of the "how" that Roshi Joan was talking about. The job didn't meet the surface "right livelihood" requirement but I created ways to make it meaningful for me, since it was the reality of my experience at that time. And I still feel good about that experience decades later, because I shifted the "why." It takes far more effort for me to drudge up the crap stories of that work, but the good ones flow freely.

Our "why" has to be more than just *"to pay my fucking bills."* Humans are story-telling creatures that must create meaning to survive. Research backs this up. People who viewed their jobs with a *"fuck it, I'm just in it for the money"* were far more likely to burn out faster than the people who have found some kind of way to align their value system to their work.

One way to keep your "why" in a good place is to remember your supporting role. This is how you find the pony in the pile of shit. Yes, you may be working for a place whose ultimate concern is profit and it's real fucking easy to feel like you sold your soul to Satan. And your employer may, empirically, be either Satan or one of her high-ranking minions.

If so, ask yourself: Who am I here to support? Usually, it's not your boss, the owners, or the shareholders. If you are providing a direct service, you're supporting the people you provide the service to. If you are a supervisor or manager, you are supporting the people who are providing services to others. That is your job . . . *period*. The money making part tends to always take care of itself when you do that.

What Can You Control About Your Livelihood?
Part of figuring out who your job is to support is knowing what is within your ability to actually do.

I like to focus on what's truly in anyone's ability to control, and use that information to shape right livelihood. So in the space below, write in what is in your control and what is outside of your control in relation to your work.

I know, there may not be much that is truly in your control outside of your own responses to work fuckery. But you can use this information to create ways in which you can create more right livelihood in your current circumstances. Maybe if your work has strict policies about destroying unsold food where you work, you

Out of My Control

In My Control

can still "throw away" food in a clean bag by putting it out by the dumpster so individuals who are hungry can find it. Or maybe it's just finding ways to remain non-reactionary to daily bullshit so you can maintain a sense of peace for yourself at work.

Do the best you can, as often as you can, for as long as you can. Until you can't.

You are not going to feel 100% every day you clock in. As much as I love my job, there are plenty of days I'd rather curl up in bed with a book or three and a cat or three. But if I'm committed to showing up, I'm not going to do a half-assed job of it. My clients, interns, students, and team members deserve the best me. (It probably also helps that one of my businesses is a publishing house I co-founded with my husband. So if I do a shitty job, he can find me pretty easily)

This sounds simple, but there may become a point where it isn't doable anymore. Your job sucks so bad, you can't find what you need inside yourself to do the best you can anymore.

And you have to be really aware of your internal signals if that's the case. Are you going through a year's worth of sick days in three months? Do you feel nausea and dread the evening before you have to go into work? Do you feel that you can't find a way to connect to your supporting role anymore? Do the people who know you best keep asking what your malfunction is?

It would be awesome to be able to torch bridges on our way out the door the minute that happens. This isn't an actual feasible option 99.44% of the time, as you well know. But start to plan your escape route. Even if you have to dig out that wall for years on end like you are Tim Robbins in The Shawshank Redemption, you will find being there far more tolerable every day that you're digging. Having a plan can really help with those (very real and very legitimate) feelings of helplessness and powerlessness.

In 2015, Researchers at Gallup conducted a poll which found that 70% of the people who were struggling to feel engaged in their jobs felt that way because of their bosses. Further, 50% of the people who quit their job did so because of those bosses.

Often it's not your boss making you miserable, but your coworkers, and while that is not easy, it is often a little easier to cope with. One of the most freeing moments in my career was when I finally ceased to give a shit about people being shitty at their jobs as long as they weren't impeding mine. My general philosophy ever since has been "be helpful or move outta my way" and it sure made things more tolerable. Just imagine yourself putting these people in the corner with a juice box and some crayons. They can color while the adults are working.

Other people's incompetence isn't your problem, unless you are their supervisor, in which case you already have the power to do something about it. If it's really affecting your ability to do your job, that's when you need to have a convo with their actual supervisor. Otherwise it's their problem and not yours.

And if you are a supervisor? Owning your bullshit, taking responsibility, and apologizing will buy you more devotion from your employees than a badass salary and a basket of muffins. If you step in with a "'That was my call, she was acting on my authority, so this conversation should be between us, not you and her" or you say "That didn't work, and I really appreciate everyone trying to make it work. Let's look at new options, what do y'all think?" then people will know that (a) you aren't trying to be a dick, (b) you aren't gonna throw them under the bus, (c) you actually give a shit about them and their work, and (d) you really are trying to do a good job.

Wanna be the go-to person? Produce whatever needs to be produced. Whether you are a supervisor or not, you can still lead by example. No one ever busted my chops about bathroom cleaning or dish washing duty when I was managing a sandwich shop because I was in the same rotation for the shit jobs. And even as a colleague working at the same level, I would almost always get support from my coworkers because I was out there busting my ass as hard as I could. It takes a special kind of asshole to not up their game when you've upped yours. Yeah, I know those motherfuckers exist, but most people rise to the occasion, if only because you just publicly shamed them into doing so.

I once had a truly heinous coworker. But by this point I'd learned enough to not take her meanness personally. I could see she was horrible to everyone, therefore it wasn't about me. And in terms of our jobs, we worked together just fine but most importantly? She had zero effect on my self-worth. This is not just a job lesson, this is a life lesson. There are very few people who know me and love me well enough that if they were shitty to me it would really hurt. And it would hurt because it meant something was seriously wrong between us. My list is a pretty small list and yours probably should be as well. And if a colleague or supervisor is on it, it should only be because they are also a mentor who is equally invested in their relationship with you.

This doesn't mean that you shouldn't feel bad if you genuinely upset someone and their upset-ness is well deserved. You should apologize authentically, rectify whatever you can, and don't do the shitty thing again to the best of your ability. Own your fuck-ups. But even then their upset-ness isn't something you should carry around as a soul wound. This shouldn't smash you in the solar plexus. And if this upset person has an upset-ness that has zero to do with your actions? Then this doesn't need to be carried by you at all. Figure out who is on your list, and remind yourself of this when people NOT on the list are getting to you.

Asking for a Raise

It's easy to get frustrated with how it seems that everyone gets jobs or moves up in their workplace anymore. And if you are reading this, you likely aren't the boss's kid, therefore are not one of those people with a leg up to move up. And when that's the case it's easy to think you have no fucks in your pocket because you can't compete at that level. But if you DON'T have a Daddy Moneybags to hook you up, the only thing you DO have is your ability to kick ass. I've always preferred the person who worked hard and was eager to learn than the person who was wicked-smart and thought that everything going on was beneath them.

And while you're working your butt off, you can also (and generally should!) ask for raises at your current job. A lot of the same advice from the chapter on salary negotiation applies. What are the raise possibilities or the "extra" possibilities if the dollar bills aren't available?

As someone who has been both the ask-er and the ask-ee, I can tell you that you will have far more success if you are very specific and to the point, and have data available to prove your point. There is nothing more fucking frustrating than needing something basic to be successful at your job and being told "NEIN," right? And, true story, some places are going to be total dick-faces no matter what you ask for . . . like a bathroom break and a 3-cent raise will make you uniquely responsible for the downfall of Western civilization.

But that doesn't mean it isn't worth asking, and you might be surprised by what you are able to get.

How you request a raise matters. A friend of mine recently sent me the draft of his raise request to edit before he sent it . . . and it was completely full of information that wasn't important to the initial ask. He mentioned performance feedback he had received from on-site supervisors and peers in great detail (which might come up in negotiations but was too much for the initial ask) and went into great detail about how he had moved out of town and was incurring additional travel expenses to come into town for his shifts (And honestly? That was not his boss's problem).

The one he actually sent after I slashed it to bits was:

> *"I have been with the organization since 2015 and have received the same per diem in compensation since that time. Last year, I completed my PhD, and would like to discuss an increase in my pay rate that reflects my current level of education and experience with the organization. Can we set aside some time to discuss options in the next couple of weeks?"*

Then he went into that meeting with specific numbers in mind, as well as other potential benefits like paid trainings. He made the discussion about the goals and values he shared with the organization. Just as we both guessed, the money wasn't there to increase his salary, but his boss did start applying for grants that helped cover further training and certifications that he was planning on investing in anyway. More money would have been ideal, but the solution they came up with went far into managing my friend's frustration and resentment over his stunted compensation.

Leaving Your Crappy Job

When you finally are ready to leave, don't take a crap (literally or metaphorically) on your boss's desk on your way out the door (even if this practice constitutes my husband's sole suggestion for this chapter). Even if you know there is no fuckingbloodyhell way you would ever work there again, you can be honest about why you are leaving without stooping to their toolbox level while doing so.

The kinds of things to say:

1) I had many good experiences working there, but ultimately, I found that many of the things I was hoping to accomplish didn't mesh with the goals of the organization.

2) I think the organization is in a rebuilding phase right now and will be in a really good place in the future. I worked with some amazing people, and I know they will continue to do amazing things there.

3) I left for very specific reasons (they included, XYZ). These reasons are about me, not about the company in its entirety or everyone that works there.

And I promise you, people will get it. They will totally know what you are saying (especially if you work for a place that's well known for their dickitude) and future employers will love the fact that you don't shit-talk former employers. When I drop one of those lines, usually people laugh and say "Gotcha. Thanks." And we move on, both understanding what was left unsaid.

And you may find yourself bumping up against those former employers again, and having left gracefully may pay off in spades. (I've actually done contract work for companies I have left. It allowed me to effect real change when being an employee there did not. And I could do that because I never trashed them publicly when we both knew I could have.) It has also allowed me the Plan Z of going back to work there if I ever needed a job on the quick. My reputation with them was intact. Sometimes the job market dictates having to eat a little crow in order to keep a roof over your head.

The side hustle: friend or foe?

Side hustles are a reality for most of us. The extra money can be used for a lot of things: to make ends meet; to be able to save for a trip; to get ahead of our debt. All that important shit. They allow flexibility in a system that doesn't support a fuller range of choices for most people.

Maybe your side hustle is extra on top of your regular job. Maybe it's what's helping you get by at all, or maybe it's helping you save up for the security to take a big leap.

Maybe your side hustle is your main hustle, allowing you to be home for your kids, or care for an ailing partner, or have the flexibility to work on your music, or manage your chronic illness. And while the hellscape aspects of the gig economy continue to frustrate me, I also appreciate that the flexibility can be an important trade-off.

Or maybe your income is cobbled together from various side hustles, for money and barter. For many years (and before Silicon Valley got involved in the gig economy), I was the side hustle queen because I had two small children and couldn't afford to work (day care expenses in the U.S. are ridiculous, in case any of my readers in more progressive countries are wondering).

The important thing is to consider how much time we have to devote to side hustles, and choosing stuff that won't burn us out even further.

I work with a couple who started doing some food delivery gigs together a few times a month to save up for a vacation. Only one of them was "earning" the money, but they went together. One drove and the other navigated and they spent time together, and really enjoyed themselves, listened to music, connected with each other at the end of a long week . . . and maybe they could have made more money doing separate things, but then they would have been isolated in their own hustle. The extra money was important to them, but not at the expense of their relationship. So they found it was something they looked *forward* to. Once they didn't need that extra money anymore, they found they still prioritized spending that extra time together and planned other things to do, like going to the zoo. I love how they turned the whole experience into a really great one.

Also? You don't need to work for one of these giant corporations to get your side hustle on. People have been side hustling since capitalism was invented. Since adulthood (nevermind all my kiddo side hustles like babysitting and the like), I have done the following:

making baked goods for events and parties, making and selling jewelry, writing content for websites, doing online tutoring, teaching part time, consulting part time, and hey . . . writing books may be the ultimate badass side hustle but it totally is one. Maybe you have a skill or hobby that you can use to supplement your income, or to barter for things you might not be able to buy. That's an important thing to consider as you plan to budget for your goals.

If you are looking at side hustles as a possibility, it's important to invest some time and research into it, just like you would any money making endeavors. There are plenty of shit-show situations that you will want to avoid. And honestly, for my creative peeps, it's important to consider whether monetizing the things you love will end up ruining them. We'll get to all that in a second.

Side Hustle Homework

- List out all the potential side hustles you've thought about.

- Google for more side hustle ideas. Anything sound interesting that you hadn't thought of? Bonus points for fun and/or rewarding.

- Rank out the few that seem the most intriguing.

- Research what the up-front investment cost would be.

- And do some research on how much money people are *actually* making.

- What about the time factor? How much time could you devote to this project without damaging your physical and mental health or having to de-prioritize your relationships or other important stuff?

- What will be your next step?

Make Sure Your Side Hustle Isn't a Trap

Unfortunately, there are a lot of potential side hustles out there that end up costing you money instead of making you money. And we are all prone to optimistically jumping into them without doing our homework first. This can be anything from gig work to self-publishing services to multi-level marketing schemes to straight-up scams. Check out the list of questions at the end of this section to screen for potential opportunities to make sure you aren't going to be hustling against your own bottom line.

The gig economy—aka large app-based companies that pay you a fee to offer rides, rent rooms in your home, deliver food, or do odd jobs—can work out ok, but it isn't always a good deal for you. Often these gigs come with upfront investments, or external costs—like using your own car—make sure you fully understand these costs before committing.

One thing to 100% avoid, no matter what: multi-level marketing (MLM) programs (also called network marketing) are nothing more than pyramid schemes, where you don't make the bulk of the money from selling a product, , but from you signing other people up under you to sell those products.

The model didn't start with inherently evil intentions. Fun fact: Avon was started in 1886. The idea was selling perfume door to door. This was a time when women generally couldn't go to stores to smell and try on perfumes. And a woman of color? Even if you could get to a department store, you weren't allowed in. Avon allowed women access to products and a way of producing income and starting their own businesses. This is all empowering, liberating stuff.

But companies with this business model have morphed into sketch-ass shenanigans that prey on the trust and good faith of a wide range of people, not just people that are desperately poor or uneducated. A 2018 survey by the AARP found that about one in thirteen people have participated in an MLM. And the number of people who have lost money in these programs, sometimes up to *tens of thousands* of dollars? According to a study by the Federal Trade Commission, it was 99% of participants. And that's not even counting the value of their invested time.

The companies make false and misleading claims, preying on people's financially traumatized brains. The aforementioned FTC fined one of the biggest offenders, Herbalife, with a $200 million fine for just such shenanigans in 2017.

And yet they still abound. Household products, body care products, clothes, candles, sex toys. If in any other area in your life someone asked you to drop several thousands of dollars with a minute chance of making a return on that investment you would laugh your ass off. So research the fuck out of any of these "make money" deals that you bump into.

Is it a networked type event? Did you go to someone's wine and cheese party and then get pitched for a product? All the nopes. Pile your pockets with as much cheese as you can, pour the wine into the water tumbler you carry with you, and peace the fuck out.

If you've been solicited to start a "home based business" or "make money working from home," look the company up. What does the Better Business Bureau say? Are there any Attorney General filed grievances? Easiest way to scope something like this out? Google "complaints about *X* company" and look for patterns of problems. If you find them? Peace the fuck out on the investment. You can also check out www.isthisanmlm.com and PinkTruth.com for hard facts and figures about MLMs.

MLMs are not side hustles, they're the fucking devil.

If you find that you *have* been caught up in a scam or just a really bad deal, be compassionate with yourself. Also, get out of there as soon as you realize you've been had—no need to throw more money away.

If you're really tempted by a side hustle opportunity that doesn't pencil out when you ask the questions below, spend some time thinking about what appeals to you most. Is it the type of work? The flexible schedule and work from home? The promise of big money? Go back to the drawing board and make a plan for how to pursue these needs and interests in your current job or in a new job. These are all possible things for you, and you'll get there faster without having to financially recover from learning the MLM lesson the hard way.

Is it a Legit Side Hustle or Is it a Pyramid Scheme?

Take a long hard look at the side hustle you're looking to start and answer these questions about it to figure out if it's a real side-hustle or if it's a pyramid scheme masquerading as #Boss #ShowThatHustle #Empowerment.

Early possible red flags: Being recruited by another distributor (like at a house party or someone you haven't talked to since high school DMing you). Being told it's "direct sales" and that it's a work from home job with flexible hours and high income potential. Anything that sounds cheerfully vague. Being told your investment will grow quickly. Being rushed into a decision. Only finding the costs in the finest of fine print. The company is brand new. The company wants you to work for equity.

Ask these questions and take notes on the answers:

- What is the upfront cost or investment?

- What are the recurring costs?

- How are you paid? How often? Do you have to hit a certain threshold for payout?

- Are refunds for unsold products standard practice?

- What are the highest, lowest, and most likely amounts of income you could reasonably make in your first month? What are the statistical chances of someone earning at each of those levels?

- How much time will you need to invest in your first month in order to make the least and most likely income levels? How much does that pencil out hourly?

- Can you afford the worst case scenario from doing this?

- Is it multi-level? Meaning, would you make more money by recruiting other people than by selling the products themselves?

- What kinds of caveats or complaints do you see when you look the company up? What does the Better Business Bureau have to say about them? Google Reviews?

- Imagine telling the most adult, responsible person in your life about this opportunity (or actually tell them)—what's their reaction?

Putting Your Creativity to Work

Sometimes the best side hustle is the thing you are doing anyway, purely for the love of it.

Us creative types run into a dilemma about this on the regular: should we monetize our joy? Whether as a career or a side hustle, the question becomes . . . if there is something that we absolutely love doing, if this is something that feeds us and heals us and makes life worth living, should we make money off that process? Are we tainting or destroying something sacred if we do? Will we ruin it for ourselves in the process?

The act of creation is far more emotional than intellectual isn't it? It's how we make sense of ourselves and the world around us. It's how we communicate to other people and make our own internal processes known to ourselves.

But that doesn't mean it's bougie or uncouth or *unartistic* to monetize your art.

If you haven't seen Amanda Palmer's TED Talk on the art of asking, go look that shit up and watch it. You can absolutely do it right now. I'll stay put and wait for you to do that and come back.

You're back? Cool. Amanda Palmer's main point is that if you *give*, you are allowed to *receive*. And creative works ARE a form of giving. *Culture is anything we create.* I mean, you can have a more academic-y definition of what culture is, but that's mine. And the act of creation shapes not just us, but everyone else who comes in contact with it. And that exchange becomes a relationship. When Amanda was asked how she was able to make people pay for her music, she responded:

> *"I didn't make them. I'd connected with them, and when you connect with people, they want to help you. It's kind of counterintuitive for a lot of artists."*

As we become more mindful and aware of the negative impacts of the industrialization of commodities and everything they are used to produce, many of us are shifting towards supporting growers, developers, and creators directly. We are moving back to more direct relationships in which we develop relationships with others and support their work because of the *relationship* as much as the work itself.

This is all to say, monetizing your joy doesn't make you a sell-out if you do it with this level of mindfulness. It means you have the capacity to impact the economy like the seriously badass, punk-rock creator that you are.

But being mindful also means *you don't have to* create something for sale just because you can. Humans are wired to create because it is another form of story-telling . . . and we definitely know that we are wired to story-tell (this is where I refer back to my book *Unfuck Your Brain*, if you haven't read it yet). Creativity has enormous long and short term mental health benefits. Numerous studies demonstrate engaging in creative endeavors helps to manage both physical and emotional pain. And you don't have to monetize the thing that keeps you whole. Or you don't have to monetize it in ways that do not align with your values.

Which brings us back, entirely, to Joan Halifax's interpretation of right livelihood. The what and why are important, but so is the how. And figuring out that part ahead of time, before your knee-deep in a pile of art supplies.

1) What's your joy? Meaning, what's your creative outlet that people keep telling you "OMG YOU SHOULD TOTALLY SELL THOSE I WOULD BUY THEM?" (if you have shown other people, anyway).

2) What would be the benefits of doing so?

3) What would be the possible downside?

4) What kind of investment would you need to make in order to start (not just financial investment in supplies and the like, but investment in your time and energy, too)

5) Is that an investment that would make sense in your life right now?

6) How would you measure success in this enterprise? (e.g., I'm enjoying myself, I make at least X amount of money per craft show I do, etc.)

7) How would you know that you want to discontinue this effort? (e.g., I'm losing sleep to keep up with the workload, I am having to undervalue my work to match the current market, etc.)

Conclusion

Shit. Ok. So.

This is the part where I give you a big motivational pep-talk about how you totally got this shit down cold and you are gonna be a money bad-ass and retire before age 40 and spend the rest of your years rescuing pygmy goats and eating ginger cookies.

I mean, I'm down.

But we are calling it a capitalist hellscape for a reason. It is one. The financial structure of modern society is a a fucking late-stage dumpster fire.

I would love to be writing about universal basic income (which pilot programs are showing to be incredibly successful). About decolonization and food sovereignty (same). About universal housing and healthcare (same same).

About how we can absolutely afford it, we just haven't prioritized it.

Case in point: The funding campaign to restore Notre Dame after the fire, found jillionaires pledging far more than even the uppermost end of the estimates for repair were going to cost within days of the start of the campaign. And I'm not saying we shouldn't repair Notre Dame, I'm saying the fucking money is out there to fix literally all of these problems.

I'm not writing about those issues, because there are scholars in those areas who are screaming from the rooftops already about those issues. And running for office. And planting gardens. And I'm reading their books, voting my ass off for them, donating to their causes, and doing everything else to support the enormous sea-change we need to undertake.

But that isn't this book. Because this book is about the *"in the meantime."* It's about the emotional consequences of the hellscape and how to cope with them in a continuously fucked up situation. Likely none of us are retiring early to hang with the pygmy goats or travel the world.

But we can all work to be as OK as possible in a really shitty situation. To recognize what's going on so we can make better decisions. More proactive and less reactive.

If I want you to close this book with any kind of woo-hoo motivational pep talk, it's this one: You are not broken. You are not a failure.

The system is.

And the better we understand the system, the better we can operate within it. Hack it. Depersonalize our experience of it so we can see the underlying mechanisms of the whole thing. You know, survive to fight another day. Decouple our worth from our wallet. Create a life worth living, come hell or high water.

Shit. I guess that was kinda motivational-peppy after all.

Fuck it then . . . let's go.

References

5 Psychology Findings That Affect Career Decisions. (n.d.). Retrieved from https://www.thecareerpsychologist.com/10-psychology-findings-that-affect-career-decisions-1-5/

8 Examples of "Mental Accounting" and How to Avoid Them. (2017, February 7). Retrieved from https://thecollegeinvestor.com/8748/examples-of-mental-accounting/

AARP Study of Multilevel Marketing. https://www.aarp.org/content/dam/aarp/aarp_foundation/2018/pdf/AARP Foundation MLM Research Study Report 10.8.18.pdf.

Allegretto, S., & Cooper, D. (n.d.). Twenty-Three Years and Still Waiting for Change: Why It's Time to Give Tipped Workers the Regular Minimum Wage. Retrieved from https://www.epi.org/publication/waiting-for-change-tipped-minimum-wage/

Are You Struggling With Financial PTSD? (2019, June 19). Retrieved from https://goop.com/work/money/are-you-struggling-with-financial-ptsd/

Ariely D. and Kreisler J. (2017). Dollars and Sense. NY: HarperCollins Publisher

Beck, J. S., & Beck, J. S. (2011). Cognitive therapy: basics and beyond. New York: Guilford Press.

Berger, J. (2019). Invisible Influence: the hidden forces that shape behaviour. S.l.: SIMON & SCHUSTER LTD.

Black D. W. (2007). A review of compulsive buying disorder. World Psychiatry 6 14–18.

Black, D.W. Mol Diag Ther (2001) 15: 17. https://doi.org/10.2165/00023210-200115010-00003

Blanco, Moreyra, & J, S.-R. (n.d.). Department of Psychiatry, Columbia University/New York State Psychiatric Institute, New York, NY 10032, USA. cb255@columbia.edu. Retrieved from https://europepmc.org/abstract/med/11447568

Bloom, S. L. (2012). Trauma-Organized Systems. Encyclopedia of Trauma. C. R. Figley. Thousand Oaks, CA, Sage: 741-743.

Bond, Casey. "5 Signs It's Time For You To Hire A Financial Planner." HuffPost, HuffPost, 12 Oct. 2018, https://www.huffpost.com/entry/when-should-hire-financial-advisor-cost_n_5bbbd47ae4b0876edaa0fc53

Bond, Casey. "Here's What It Actually Takes To Change Your Money Habits." HuffPost, HuffPost, 9 May 2019, https://www.huffpost.com/entry/get-better-with-money-habits_l_5cd30aa9e4b0a7dffcd0416d.

Bridgman, B.; Andrew Dugan; Mikhael Lal; Matthew Osborne & Shaunda Villones (2012), Accounting for Household Production in the National Accounts (PDF), p. 2

Bronfenbrenner, U. (1979). The ecology of human development. Cambridge, MA. Harvard University Press.

Campbell, A. F. (2018, August 24). The federal government markets prison labor to businesses as the "best-kept secret". Retrieved from https://www.vox.com/2018/8/24/17768438/national-prison-strike-factory-labor

Carroll, M., & Carroll, M. (2019, July 24). My Livelihood Doesn't Seem Right. Retrieved from https://www.lionsroar.com/my-livelihood-doesnt-seem-right/.

Chapter 7: MLM's ABYSMAL NUMBERS - Ftc.gov. https://www.ftc.gov/sites/default/files/documents/public_comments/trade-regulation-rule-disclosure-requirements-and-prohibitions-concerning-business-opportunities-ftc.r511993-00008 /00008-57281.pdf.

Chunn, L. (2017, May 10). The psychology of the to-do list – why your brain loves ordered tasks. Retrieved from https://www.theguardian.com/lifeandstyle/2017/may/10/the-psychology-of-the-to-do-list-why-your-brain-loves-ordered-tasks

Collins, K., Connors, K., Davis, S., Donohue, A., Gardner, S., Goldblatt, E., Hayward, A., Kiser, L., Strieder, F. Thompson, E. (2010). Understanding the impact of trauma and urban poverty on family systems: Risks, resilience, and interventions. Baltimore, MD: Family Informed Trauma Treatment Center. http://nctsn.org/nccts/nav.do?pid=ctr_rsch_prod_ar or http://fittcenter.umaryland.edu/WhitePaper.asp

Cahill, S. P., & Foa, E. B. (2007). Psychological theories of PTSD. In M. J. Friedman, T. M. Keane, & P. A. Resick (Eds.), Handbook of PTSD: Science and practice (pp. 55-77). New York: The Guilford Press.

Chatzky, J. (2018, November 10). Why we spend money on things we shouldn't (and how to break the cycle). Retrieved from https://www.nbcnews.com/better/business/why-we-spend-money-things-we-shouldn-t-how-break-ncna930616

Clark, A. F., Barrett, L., & Kolvin, I. (2000). Inner city disadvantage and family functioning. European Child & Adolescent Psychiatry, 9(2), 77-83.

Clifford, S. (2011, August 17). Abercrombie Wants Off 'Jersey Shore' (Wink-Wink). Retrieved from https://www.nytimes.com/2011/08/18/business/abercrombie-offers-jersey-shore-cast-a-paid-non-product-placement.html

Conger, R. D., Wallace, L. E., Sun, Y., Simons, R. L., McLoyd, V., & Brody, G. H. (2002). Economic pressure in African American families: A replication and extension of the family stress model. Developmental Psychology, 38, 179-193.

Consumer Financial Protection Bureau (CFPB), Financial well-being in America September 2017,http://files.consumerfinance.gov/f/documents/201709_cfpb_financial-well-being-in-America.pdf

"Credit and Debt Advice." NFCC, https://www.nfcc.org/

Deurzen, van, et al. "Income Inequality and Depression: The Role of Social Comparisons and Coping Resources." OUP Academic, Oxford University Press, 12 Mar. 2015, academic.oup.com/esr/article/31/4/477/496590

Dinardo, K. (2019, October 9). The Green Revolution Spreading Across Our Rooftops. Retrieved from https://www.nytimes.com/2019/10/09/realestate/the-green-roof-revolution.html.

Empowerment Through Soji, The Simple Zen Practice of Cleaning. (2019, May 23). Retrieved from https://www.jonbernie.org/2019/05/22/empowerment-through-soji-the-simple-zen-practice-of-cleaning/

Engagement A Brief Review of - Assets.publishing.service . . . https://assets.publishing.service.gov.uk/government/uploads/system/uploads/attachment_data/file/215465/dh_129661.pdf

Evans, G.W., & English, K. (2002). The environment of poverty: Multiple stressor exposure, psychophysiological stress, and socioemotional adjustment. Child Development, 73(4), 1238-1248.

EurekAlertAAAS. (2006, April 14). Other people influence us and we don't even know it. Retrieved from https://www.eurekalert.org/pub_releases/2006-04/bpl-opi041406.php

Frederick, S. Novemsky, N. Wang, J., Dhar, R., Nowlis, S., Opportunity Cost Neglect, Journal of Consumer Research, Volume 36, Issue 4, December 2009, Pages 553–561, https://doi.org/10.1086/599764

Gammage, Sarah (September 9, 2010). "Time Pressed and Time Poor: Unpaid Household Work in Guatemala". Feminist Economics. 16 (3): 79–112. doi:10.1080/13545701.2010.498571

"GINI Index (World Bank Estimate)." Data, data.worldbank.org/indicator/SI.POV.GINI.

Graaf, J. D., Wann, D., & Naylor, T. H. (2014). Affluenza: how overconsumption is killing us-- and how we can fight back. San Francisco: Berrett-Koehler Publishers, Inc.

Gregoire, C. (2017, December 7). This Is Your Brain On Money. Retrieved from https://www.huffpost.com/entry/psychology-of-wealth_n_4531905

Hardekopf, Bill. "Do People Really Spend More With Credit Cards?" Forbes, Forbes Magazine, 16 July 2018, https://www.forbes.com/sites/billhardekopf/2018/07/16/do-people-really-spend-more-with-credit-cards/#736f44c61c19

Harkin, T., Warren, E., Dean, H., Gutierrez, L., Schultz, D. W., Trump, D., . . . Facebook. (n.d.). PolitiFact - Can employers actually pay disabled Americans below the minimum wage? Retrieved from https://www.politifact.com/factchecks/2016/aug/12/tom-harkin/can-employers-actually-pay-disabled-americans-belo/

"Herbalife International of America, Inc., Et Al." Federal Trade Commission, 8 May 2019, https://www.ftc.gov/enforcement/cases-proceedings/142-3037/herbalife-international-america-inc-et-al.

"How Art and Creativity Can Improve Your Health." Medical News Today, MediLexicon International, 16 Feb. 2018, https://www.medicalnewstoday.com/articles/320947.php.

How to Make the 50/20/30 Budgeting Method Work for You. (2014, December 16). Retrieved from https://www.mint.com/budgeting-3/how-to-make-the-502030-budgeting-method-work-for-you.

"Income Inequality." Inequality.org, inequality.org/facts/income-inequality/

Jabr, F. (2013, November 1). How the Brain Gets Addicted to Gambling. Retrieved from https://www.scientificamerican.com/article/how-the-brain-gets-addicted-to-gambling/

Kahneman, D., & Tversky, A. (1977). Prospect Theory. An Analysis of Decision Making Under Risk. doi: 10.21236/ada045771

Katz, D. (n.d.). Psychic Income. Retrieved from https://www.fa-mag.com/news/psychic-income-17033.html.

King, L. A. (n.d.). The Health Benefits of Writing about Life Goals - Laura A. King, 2001. Retrieved from https://journals.sagepub.com/doi/abs/10.1177/0146167201277003

Kiser, L. J., & Black, M. A. (2005). Family processes in the midst of urban poverty. Aggression and Violent Behavior, 10(6), 715-750.

Kiser, L. J., Ostoja, E., Pruitt, D. B. (1998) Dealing with stress and trauma in families. Stress in Children. Child and Adolescent Psychiatric Clinics of North America, 7(1), 87-104.

Kraus, Michael W., et al. "The Misperception of Racial Economic Inequality - Michael W. Kraus, Ivuoma N. Onyeador, Natalie M. Daumeyer, Julian M. Rucker, Jennifer A. Richeson, 2019." SAGE Journals, journals.sagepub.com/doi/full/10.1177/1745691619863049.

Kraus, M. W., & Keltner, D. (2013). Social class rank, essentialism, and punitive judgment. Journal of Personality and Social Psychology, 105(2), 247-261.

http://dx.doi.org/10.1037/a0032895

Loveday, Paula & Lovell, Geoff & Jones, Christian. (2016). The Best Possible Selves Intervention: A Review of the Literature to Evaluate Efficacy and Guide Future Research. Journal of Happiness Studies. 10.1007/s10902-016-9824-z.

Money Ruining Marriages in America: A Ramsey Solutions study. (n.d.). Retrieved from https://www.daveramsey.com/pr/money-ruining-marriages-in-america

Morse, Felicity. Give a f**k: a Brief Inventory of Ways in Which You Can. IXIA Press, 2019.

Mcewen, B., & Wingfield, J. (2007). Allostasis and Allostatic Load. Encyclopedia of Stress, 135–141. doi: 10.1016/b978-012373947-6.00025-8

Mental Accounting: Our Motivations Behind Spending and Saving. (2015, July 23). Retrieved from http://echelonim.com/mental-accounting/

Mitchell, J., Crosbya, R., & Zwaanc, M. (2006, February 7). Cognitive behavioral therapy for compulsive buying disorder. Retrieved from https://www.sciencedirect.com/science/article/abs/pii/S0005796705002767?via=ihub.

Morningstar.com. "Morningstar Sustainability Rating." Morningstar, Inc., 24 Aug. 2016, https://www.morningstar.com/articles/745467/morningstar-sustainability-rating.

National Center Against Domestic Violence. Domestic Violence Facts Available at: http://www.ncadv.org/files/DomesticViolenceFactSheet(National).pdf National Center for Children in Poverty. Basic Facts about Low-Income Children Birth to Age 18, October 2008. Available at: http://www.nccp.org/publications/pub_845.html

Nartey, Clara, et al. "Making The Decision To Monetize Your Creative Work: CLARA NARTEY: Unlock Your Creative Potential." CLARA NARTEY |Unlock Your Creative Potential, 10 May 2017, https://claranartey.com/monetize-your-creative-work/.

"Naylor Association Management Software." The Forum for Sustainable and Responsible Investment, Naylor Association Management Software, https://www.ussif.org/sribasics.

Neff, K. (2015). Self-compassion: stop beating yourself up and leave insecurity behind. New York: William Morrow.

Olen, H. (2016, May 26). Your Latte Isn't Why You're in Debt, and the People Who Say It Is Are Lying to You. Retrieved from https://slate.com/business/2016/05/the-latte-is-a-lie-and-buying-coffee-has-nothing-to-do-with-debt-an-excerpt-from-helaine-olens-pound-foolish.html

Olmsted, Jennifer C. (2005). "Is paid work the (only) answer? Neoliberalism, Arab women's well-being, and the social contract". Journal of Middle East Women's Studies. 1 (2): 112–139. doi:10.1215/15525864-2005-2005

O'Shea, B., Pyles, S., O'Shea, B., Bev, Pyles, S., Pyles, S., . . . New York Times. (2019, February 28). Debt avalanche or debt snowball, what's your type? Retrieved from https://www.nerdwallet.com/blog/finance/what-is-a-debt-avalanche/

Patel, Vikram, et al. "Income Inequality and Depression: a Systematic Review and Meta-Analysis of the Association and a Scoping Review of Mechanisms." World Psychiatry : Official Journal of the World Psychiatric Association (WPA), John Wiley and Sons Inc., Feb. 2018, www.ncbi.nlm.nih.gov/pmc/articles/PMC5775138/

Published: Mar 31, 2019. (2019, April 1). Where Are States Today? Medicaid and CHIP Eligibility Levels for Children, Pregnant Women, and Adults. Retrieved from https://www.kff.org/medicaid/fact-sheet/where-are-states-today-medicaid-and-chip/

Ramsey Solutions. (2019, September 23). How the Debt Snowball Method Works. Retrieved from https://www.daveramsey.com/blog/how-the-debt-snowball-method-works.

Romero, Eliza. "Why Joining An MLM Will Ruin Your Life." Medium, Noteworthy - The Journal Blog, 6 Apr. 2019, https://blog.usejournal.com/why-are-people-still-defending-mlms-c1d6ea878f83.

Schimmack, U & Lucas, R. (2007) Schmollers Jahrbuch : Journal of Applied Social Science Studies / Zeitschrift für Wirtschafts- und Sozialwissenschaften, vol. 127, issue 1, 105-111

Schroeder, Robert. "Green Party's Jill Stein Defends Big Oil Fund Investments after 'Smear Attack'." MarketWatch, 28 Oct. 2016, https://www.marketwatch.com/story/green-partys-jill-stein-defends-big-oil-fund-investments-after-smear-attack-2016-10-28.

Scott, R., DeSantis, R., Nelson, B., Putnam, A., Gillum, A., DeSantis, R., . . . Committee. (n.d.). PolitiFact - Claims about prison price-gouging decry $17 soup, $18 tampons. Retrieved from https://www.politifact.com/article/2018/jan/22/claims-about-prison-price-gouging-decry-17-soup-18/

Segal, W. K. and T. (2019, August 19). Mental Accounting Definition. Retrieved from https://www.investopedia.com/terms/m/mentalaccounting.asp

Seligman, M. E. P. (2018). Learned optimism. London: Nicholas Brealey Publishing.

Seven facts about tipped workers and the tipped minimum wage. (n.d.). Retrieved from https://www.epi.org/blog/seven-facts-about-tipped-workers-and-the-tipped-minimum-wage/

Shonin, E., Gordon, W.V., & Griffiths, M.D. (2013). Buddhist philosophy for the treatment of problem gambling. Journal of behavioral addictions, 2 2, 63-71.

Soga, M., Gaston, K. J., & Yamaura, Y. (2016, November 14). Gardening is beneficial for health: A meta-analysis. Retrieved from https://www.sciencedirect.com/science/article/pii/S2211335516301401

Staking self-worth on the pursuit of money has negative psychological consequences. (2017, April 27). Retrieved from http://www.buffalo.edu/news/releases/2017/04/046.html

Halifax, Joan. Standing at the Edge: Finding Freedom Where Fear and Courage Meet. Flatiron Books, 2019.

Sussman, A. B., & Alter, A. L. (2012). The exception is the rule: Underestimating and overspending on exceptional expenses. The Journal of Consumer Research, 39, 800–814.

Szalavitz, Maia. "Why Do We Think Poor People Are Poor Because of Their Own Bad Choices?" The Guardian, Guardian News and Media, 5 July 2017, www.theguardian.com/us-news/2017/jul/05/us-inequality-poor-people-bad-choices-wealthy-bias.

Thaler, Richard H. and Cass R. Sunstein (2008). Nudge: Improving Decisions About Health, Wealth, and Happiness. Yale University Press.

"The Center on Poverty and Inequality." Georgetown Law, www.law.georgetown.edu/poverty-inequality-center/

"The Heart Rating." Natural Investments, https://www.naturalinvestments.com/heart-rating/.

The Invisible Influence of Others. (2017, January 16). Retrieved from https://upliftconnect.com/invisible-influence-of-others/

The Median Amazon Employee's Salary Is $28,000. Jeff Bezos Makes More Than That in 10 Seconds. (n.d.). Retrieved from https://money.com/amazon-employee-median-salary-jeff-bezos/

The Science and Psychology Behind Job Search. (2020, March 6). Retrieved from http://blog.indeed.com/2015/10/22/science-behind-job-search/

"Wealth Inequality." Inequality.org, inequality.org/facts/wealth-inequality/.

Webb, K. (2018, September 17). Regulators from more than a dozen countries are looking to crack down on 'loot boxes,' a controversial video gaming practice that could be too much like gambling. Retrieved from https://www.businessinsider.com/loot-boxes-european-regulation-2018-9

"What Is a Fiduciary Financial Advisor?" U.S. News & World Report, U.S. News & World Report, https://money.usnews.com/investing/investing-101/articles/what-is-a-fiduciary-financial-advisor-a-guide-to-the-fiduciary-duty.

What Is Posttraumatic Stress Disorder? (n.d.). Retrieved from https://www.psychiatry.org/patients-families/ptsd/what-is-ptsd

What is Gambling Disorder? (n.d.). Retrieved from https://www.psychiatry.org/patients-families/gambling-disorder/what-is-gambling-disorder

Why Growing Food is The Single Most Impactful Thing You Can Do in a Corrupt Political System. (2018, April 24). Retrieved from https://realfarmacy.com/growing-food-rigged-system/.

Wiest, B. (2019, April 4). Financial Trauma Is A Reality For One Third Of Millennials, This Expert Explains How To Recover. Retrieved from https://www.forbes.com/sites/briannawiest/2019/04/04/financial-trauma-is-a-reality-for-one-third-of-millennials-this-expert-explains-how-to-recover/#10877291130c

Wilson, TD (2011) Redirect: The Surprising New Science of Psychological Change. Little, Brown and Company.

Yamamoto, Y. (2017). Allostasis, Allostatic Load. Encyclopedia of Behavioral Medicine, 1–2. doi: 10.1007/978-1-4614-6439-6_1627-2

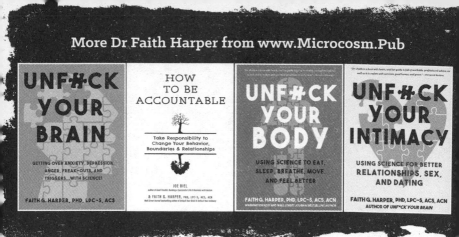